Live Free, Stay Free

 *Keys to Freedom*

Keys to Freedom Study Guide by Mercy Multiplied Intl
Published by Mercy Multiplied
P.O. Box 111060
Nashville, TN 37222

www.mercymultiplied.com

This book or parts thereof may not be reproduced in any form, stored in a retrieval system, or transmitted in any form by any means—electronic, mechanical, photocopy, recording, or otherwise—without prior written permission of the publisher, except as provided by United States of America copyright law.

Unless otherwise noted, all Scripture quotations are from the Holy Bible, New International Version of the Bible. Copyright © 1973, 1978, 1984, 2011 by Biblica, Inc. Used by permission.

Scripture quotations marked NKJV are from the New King James Version of the Bible. Copyright © 1979, 1980, 1982 by Thomas Nelson, Inc., publishers. Used by permission.

Scripture quotations marked NLT are from the Holy Bible, New Living Translation, copyright © 2007. Used by permission of Tyndale House Publishers, Inc., Wheaton, IL 60189. All rights reserved.

Scripture quotations marked The Message are from The Message: The Bible in Contemporary English, copyright © 1993, 1994, 1995, 1996, 2000, 2001, 2002. Used by permission of NavPress Publishing Group.

Scripture quotations marked ESV are from the Holy Bible, English Standard Version, Copyright © 2001 by Crossway Bibles, a division of Good News Publishers. Used by permission.

Scripture quotations marked KJV are from the King James Version of the Bible.

Copyright © 2017 by Mercy Multiplied Intl

All rights reserved

Cover design by Mike Harvie

Design Director: Christian Parsons

Visit the author's website at www.MercyMultiplied.com.

International Standard Book Number: 978-0-9986485-0-7

While the author has made every effort to provide accurate telephone numbers and Internet addresses at the time of publication, neither the publisher nor the author assumes any responsibility for errors or for changes that occur after publication.

First edition

Printed in the USA

Contents

Acknowledgments	5
About this Study	7
Introduction by Nancy Alcorn	9
Setting the Stage	13
Key 1 - *Committing and Connecting to Christ*	27
Key 2 - *Renewing Your Mind*	43
Key 3 - *Healing Life's Hurts*	57
Key 4 - *Choosing to Forgive*	71
Key 5 - *Breaking Generational Patterns*	85
Key 6 - *Choosing Freedom Over Oppression*	99
Key 7 - *Maintaining Lifelong Freedom*	113
Conclusion	127
Commitment to Freedom	129
Appendix A: *"Who I Am In Christ"*	131
Appendix B: *Faulty Beliefs and Freedom Facts*	133
Appendix C: *Daily Declarations*	139

Keys to Freedom

Acknowledgments

Friends of Mercy Multiplied: Thank you for willingly sharing your stories of healing for use in this study guide.

All the counselors at Mercy and the young women who have come through the program: Thank you for being the model and example of how these principles work and for encouraging and inspiring all of us through your stories of freedom and restoration.

Arianna Walker, Melanie Wise, and Jen Otero: Thank you for your tireless work in writing, editing, and building this study guide so that many more people will find freedom!

Ren Harvey: Thank you for allowing us to include your original artwork within the pages of this study. It provides powerful visuals for which we are so grateful.

Christy Singleton: Thank you for providing an invaluable sounding board for key points in this study guide.

Joel Kilpatrick: This study guide would not have been possible without you first pushing Nancy Alcorn to dig deep and share the principles of freedom in her book, *Ditch the Baggage*. Thank you for your expertise and belief in our mission.

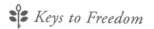

About this Study

The *Keys to Freedom* study is a valuable tool for you to discover the keys to living free and staying free in Jesus Christ. It is perfectly suited for personal study, but this book can also be used in a one-on-one or group setting. Group leader and mentor guides are available at **www.MercyMultiplied.com/KeysToFreedom**.

This study is very interactive as well. You will see a lot of blank space on the following pages because we want this to be a journey in which you are very engaged! You will be asked to look up passages in the Bible and will be challenged to ask God how He wants you to apply the principles in your own life.

At the beginning of each week's study, you will read a testimony from an individual who has personal experience with the specific week's topic. The purpose of these testimonies is to encourage you and give real-life examples of how the principles in this study work. When applied, we believe these principles have the ability to truly change your life, set you free, and become all God is calling you to be. We want to encourage you to take some time before you start each week's study to read these stories, and let them infuse you with encouragement and hope as you walk this journey!

You will want to set aside about fifteen to twenty minutes to complete your study each day. There are only five days of study per week, so on the remaining two days, we encourage you to go back and spend time reflecting over the concepts that seem most pertinent to you.

True healing and freedom ultimately come from God Himself, so at the end of each week's study, you will see a page designed for you to journal about the things you personally hear from God. As you complete your study each day, we encourage you to take a few minutes to go to the last page for that specific week, and write down any significant insights that God revealed to you through that day's study.

If you are doing this study with a group, please know that the things you write and share on the following pages can be as private as you desire for them to be. Although there can be much healing and freedom found in sharing your struggles with other people, please do not feel pressured to share anything that you are uncomfortable with sharing.

In the margins, you will find key statements for almost every day of the study. These are major points from the text that you may choose to focus on or even share with others. We encourage our fellow fans of social media to use #KeystoFreedom to share these valuable insights and what God is doing in your life. This will also give us a great way to stay connected!

 *Keys to Freedom*

Introduction by Nancy Alcorn

A couple of years ago, I was visiting one of the more prominent churches in a certain city and enjoying the privilege of speaking to the congregation about the work we do at Mercy Multiplied – helping young women find freedom from all kinds of painful, crazy, and mixed-up life experiences. After the service, a woman approached me with tears streaming down her cheeks: "I wish I had known about your ministry last year," she said. I've been living with the choices I made and … it's so hard." We prayed together that she would freely receive the Father's mercy for what was in her past.

Next a father came up: "It's my daughter," he said, sighing deeply. "She's on drugs and can't seem to shake it. It's wrecking her life. We worry about her night and day. She's had several abortions already, and she's scheduled to have her third or fourth abortion tomorrow. We're just desperate. Will you pray for her?"

I hear these stories everywhere I go. Be it a church, a mall, a workplace, or a restaurant, people all across the world carry untold stories of unresolved pain. "I wish I had heard this message and known about Mercy when I was going through what I went through," they often say to me. "I would have made a completely different choice and lived in freedom rather than bondage for all these years."

I can speak boldly into your situation because for more than thirty years, Mercy has worked with women, ages thirteen to twenty-eight, who struggle with the worst traumas someone can experience in life: self-harming habits, eating disorders, suicide, addictions, unplanned pregnancies, sexual abuse, violence, death of loved ones, and more. These kinds of behaviors and their causes are more common than you might expect. Though, for many of us, they can seem extreme. However, by helping women find freedom in these "extreme" situations and troubles, we believe we have discovered the Biblical pathway to freedom for everyone.

In 1 Thessalonians 3:3-5 (The Message) Paul writes, "Not that the troubles should come as any surprise to you. You've always known that we're in for this kind of thing. It's part of our calling. When we were with you, we made it quite clear that there was trouble ahead."

The "trouble ahead" is not because God is punishing us. The trouble ahead is part of our living environment, our earth, which is still struggling under the weight of sin and corruption. Trouble can come from us being the victims of other people's bad choices; it can come from our own ignorance and disobedience, and it can come through no fault of our own, sent by an enemy who comes to "kill, steal, and destroy" us (John 10:10).

But God has not abandoned us. He has provided all we need to navigate it well. This study is an opportunity to learn the tools that God has made available, through a relationship with Jesus Christ, to equip and empower us to navigate our lives in such a way that we can make progress and live in freedom!

This study is not a magic wand to wave over your situations, problems, obstacles and adversities. It's not a formula to follow that guarantees a comfortable, trouble-free life. However, it will empower and inspire you with hope. I encourage you to place your hand in God's hand and take the steps that will lead you to discover that overcoming your personal challenges is not an event but a process. It's a journey that is made up of a series of choices that bring lasting change and breakthrough.

This study is our way of taking the keys to freedom and wholeness, used within the four walls of our Mercy homes, and placing them into the hands of every person who wants to live free and stay free – young, old, male, female, new and established believers alike. We want to see more people able to navigate their lives from a place of freedom, wholeness and understanding, using the biblical tools of transformation made available by God through His Word.

As you begin, I encourage you to invest yourself fully in each week's principles, and see what the Lord does in your life. You may question whether or not these principles will really work for you, but Scripture promises that He is the one who is at work in you, "both to will and to work for His good pleasure" (Philippians 2:13). I encourage you to simply take the first step, and see what God does in your life. I believe that God will completely blow your mind with His life-transforming power, and once you have experienced it for yourself, you won't be able to contain it!

So, are you ready for change? Are you ready to pick up the keys to freedom? Are you ready to start unlocking doors in your life, moving forward into the future that God has for you? Then let's pray:

> ***Thank you Lord Jesus that you have made it possible for us to live in complete freedom and wholeness! At the very outset of this study, I pray that your Holy Spirit would infuse each page with anointing, truth, and revelation so that each reader will receive the keys to freedom he or she needs to walk in wholeness. I pray protection over each one as they work through this study. Give them courage, strength, and wisdom to know how to practically apply each key, not just for the duration of this study, but also for the rest of their lives. In Jesus' Name, Amen.***

Nancy Alcorn
Founder and President

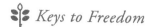

Setting the Stage

Day 1: *Getting to the Root*

Cutting off the branches won't change the fruit that grows.

One of the easiest ways to describe the approach we are going to take throughout this study is to depict our lives by using the analogy of a tree. Imagine your life as a tree with branches, a thick tree trunk and a root system underground, feeding and sustaining the tree.

The branches of this tree represent our BEHAVIORS – the "above-ground" visible aspects of who we are and how we behave. These are the things that become clear when you get to know a person well, or in some cases, the "branches" are so obvious that they can be spotted almost immediately. The branches on our tree can be healthy or unhealthy, depending on the health of our root systems. Today we will focus primarily on the unhealthy factors in our lives, as those are the things that we need to address in order to overcome.

Some very common unhealthy branches (behaviors) that can grow on the tree of our life can include things like:

- Inability to commit to relationships, a church, job, etc.
- Lack of healthy boundaries
- People-pleasing behaviors (struggling with saying no and finding self-worth through acceptance of others)
- Promiscuity
- Putting others down, comparison and feeling threatened by others' success
- Bullish/aggressive/intimidating behaviors
- Manipulation (actions that position one to stay in control of others and situations)
- Independence and self-sufficiency
- Emotional instability (either disconnected or too connected to emotions)

More serious "life-controlling" branches (behaviors) can include:

- Eating disorders
- Self-harm
- Depression
- Anxiety Disorders and Panic attacks (Insomnia, Obsessive Compulsive Disorder)
- Addictions (alcohol, drugs, pornography, social media, work, video games, etc.)

The tree trunk describes the BELIEF SYSTEM a person has developed over the course of their life. Our belief system is what sustains and upholds our behaviors. We act within the context of how we think and what we believe.

> *We act within the context of how we think and what we believe.*

The roots of the tree feed both the tree trunk and the branches. These roots draw their power from the specific circumstances that affect us from childhood, such as divorce, the loss of a loved one, long term sickness, or any other mental, spiritual, sexual or physical trauma. Interestingly, while the branches that grow on people's lives can vary tremendously from person to person, as we all have a variety of healthy and unhealthy branches, the types of roots that feed those branches tend to be fairly universal. Those roots then grow into a trunk – a belief system – and it's our belief system that determines our behaviors.

The roots listed below are some examples of "the why behind the what" – the true causes of the issues in our lives. Many of us are affected by their presence, without even realizing their influence.

- Abandonment
- Rejection
- Abuse
- Unworthiness
- Shame
- Fear
- Guilt
- Insecurity
- Pride
- Bitterness

People typically focus their attention only on what they can see, so help is sought (and given) with the "cutting off" of unhealthy branches. In other words, behavior modification is the goal, and negative behaviors are often dealt with by behavior management and/or medication. This approach may appear successful because a branch can indeed be cut off and removed from the tree; however, unless the root structure is addressed, that same branch will grow back, either in the very same place or elsewhere on the same tree. That is true for the tree that stands in a garden as much as it is true for the tree that represents your life.

Though it may seem like destructive behavior is causing the most damage in your life, the challenge is not simply a behavioral issue; rather, the challenge we all face is the removal of fundamental "root" issues. These destructive roots are at the core of our destructive behaviors. Without dealing with the roots, the behavior can never truly be healed. In many cases, our "roots" are damaged by the behaviors of imperfect people and imperfect circumstances in our lives. The truth is that we need a perfect God to bring the revelation and healing that cannot come merely by focusing on the unhealthy branches.

Consider the branches and roots operating in your life today. Try to identify 2 or 3 branches and 2 or 3 roots, and write them on the tree below. If it's difficult for you to identify these things in your life right now, don't be discouraged. They will likely become clearer to you as we move forward in the study.

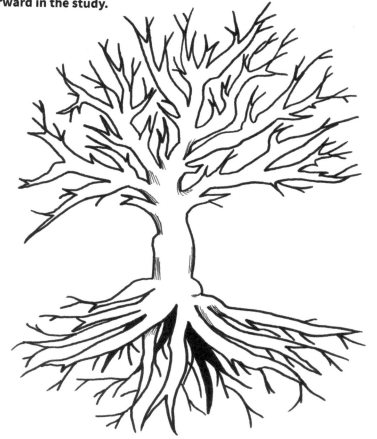

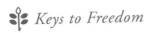 Keys to Freedom   Setting the Stage

Now that you have identified some areas on your own tree, spend some time in prayer before you close your study time. Use the space below to ask the Lord to help you in the process of overcoming any areas that you have identified today.

Day 2: *The Roots Determine the Fruit*

Yesterday we spent some time discussing the tree analogy that we will use throughout this study and the importance of recognizing the roots in our lives. As we mentioned yesterday, this is not typically the way that people address their issues. The focus is usually on addressing the behaviors themselves – the "branches" – instead of addressing the roots.

Write Matthew 12:33 in the space below.

This scripture says that a tree can be made either good or bad, and that either way, it is known by its fruit. The fruit that a tree produces cannot be affected by simply cutting off the branches. Making a tree healthy – making our lives whole, healed, and free – has to come from our roots.

Setting the Stage

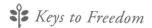 *Keys to Freedom*

If you choose to remain focused on the negative behaviors that you want to overcome instead of your past hurt, betrayal, trauma, disappointment or abuse, those roots will continue to shape your belief system, and you will continue to grow the branches of damaging and unhealthy behaviors.

> *Making a tree healthy — making our lives whole, healed and free —has to come from our roots.*

What does Jeremiah 17:7-8 say about our roots? What do we need to be fed by?

Our roots need to be fed by God's Word, His presence, and His power. The roots of abandonment, rejection, fear, anger, shame, guilt, pride, bitterness, and unworthiness will never be able to produce healthy fruit. We may be able to cut off the branches by using all of our will power and resources, but a tree without branches produces no fruit at all. It is bare, lifeless, and will not fulfill its potential and purpose.

Write out the fruit that is described in Galatians 5:22-23.

Over the coming weeks, you will have the opportunity to examine your behaviors, to rebuild your belief system with what God's Word says about you, and to receive healing for the pain that enabled those roots to grow. We are going to teach you the tools for exposing the root causes of your behaviors through a partnership with the Holy Spirit. As you focus on the root system in your life instead of the branches, you will have the opportunity to truly overcome in a whole new way!

As you wrap up your study for today, write one "fruit" that you would like to see flourish in your life. As that fruit becomes more evident in you and through you, how will your life be enriched?

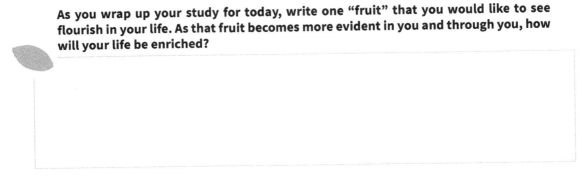

Tomorrow we will begin discussion on a topic that is not only a foundational part of this study but also for any true healing and transformation that you receive.

Day 3: *Hearing the Voice of God – Part I*

This week, we are focused on setting the stage for the rest of our study with a few foundational pieces. So far we have discussed the tree analogy and the importance of identifying and understanding the root systems in our lives, which ultimately feed our behaviors. Today we will discuss the different ways that God speaks to us as His sons and daughters.

While God speaks to us in many different ways, His primary means of communication with His people is through his Word, the Bible. The Word of God is not simply a history book or book of stories. In fact, Hebrews 4:12 tells us that the Word is actually living and active. It has the ability to change our hearts, and it always has something to say about our lives. The Word is our ultimate standard of truth.

However, Scripture is not the only way that God speaks to His children. One of the most amazing benefits of being a child of God is that we have the ability to directly communicate back and forth with Him. Today we will focus on helping you identify how you personally receive from the Lord and position you to do so throughout this study.

What does Jesus say in John 10:27?

Jesus had an expectation from the beginning that we would listen to His voice and have two-way communication with the Father through the Holy Spirit.

God can communicate to you in many different ways. It might come as a thought, a memory, a picture, or a verse from the Bible that pops into your mind. When we refer to hearing from the Lord, it does not necessarily mean that you hear an audible voice. It simply means that the Lord shows you something, and you receive what He is communicating to you. In our Mercy program, we teach the residents from the beginning of their stay that the Lord desires to communicate with them and help them identify how they most readily receive from Him.

> *Jesus had an expectation from the beginning that we would listen to His voice and have two-way communication with the Father through the Holy Spirit.*

Here are four common ways that the Lord speaks, or communicates, with us:

- **His still, small voice** – This is often referred to as our conscience, or that voice in our head, that redirects or challenges us when we are struggling with making a decision. That still, small voice is the Holy Spirit speaking to our mind and hearts. As this way of hearing from the Lord grows, you will find yourself having two-way conversations with Him throughout the day.

- **Impressions** – These are thoughts that come to mind that we do not intentionally think on our own. These thoughts seem to fall quietly as we become aware of them. Some examples of this may be an inclination to do something for someone that we did not think of on our own or a memory coming to mind that we have not thought about in a long time.

- **Confirmation** – This is when the Lord speaks through themes that are confirmed over and over again. Some people would call this "coincidence". People who receive from the Lord in this way will begin to recognize the Lord speaking a specific theme to them – for example, forgiveness – and will see it in many ways and places. One morning they may overhear a conversation about forgiveness, see a billboard with this theme across it, and then notice a license plate with 4GVNESS. Later, they might receive a flier in the mail, and then read two Bible verses on forgiveness! The theme would seem to be everywhere because the Lord doesn't mind repeating Himself or confirming what He is speaking when one of His children is open and aware.

- **Pictures** – Sometimes this is referred to as visions or dreams. This area can often sound a bit weird, or even spooky, but it is a legitimate and significant way God uses to speak to His children. Receiving from the Lord in picture form is often found in people who are creative and imaginative. They see pictures easily and may receive dreams from the Lord while they sleep as well. Sometimes the meaning of these dreams or pictures is not clear right away, but through prayer and discussion with other believers, the Lord will reveal what He was communicating with you through the dream or picture.

It's important that we understand our uniqueness when we begin to discern the ways that the Lord speaks to us. Any parent of more than one child would agree that each of their children is unique in the way they are designed, the way they communicate and learn, and the way they connect with them as parents. It is the same thing for us as sons and daughters of God. He has made us uniquely; therefore, the way we will connect with Him and hear from Him will be unique.

 Keys to Freedom

Setting the Stage

Let's take some time to identify how you most readily receive from the Lord.

In what ways do you most naturally connect with the Lord (e.g. Bible reading, worship, out in nature)?

When you are communicating with someone, do you typically see pictures, or do you hear words?

Have you ever had a thought come to mind and wondered if it was from the Lord? Perhaps an impression?

When is the last time you experienced the Lord revealing something to you? In what form did it come? What did He speak to you or show you during that moment?

The concept of hearing from the Lord may be something you are very comfortable with, or it may be something that is new information to you. We encourage you to take a few minutes and create space for the Lord to speak/reveal Himself to you. Simply ask Him, "Lord, what is one thing that You like about me?" As you receive something in prayer, write it down or draw it in the space below.

Sometimes individuals experience a "block" in their ability to hear clearly from the Lord when they begin this exercise. This block may be the result of anger, hurt, or lack of forgiveness. Other times, you may be expecting to hear from the Lord in a certain way, and He communicates with you in another. For example, if you are waiting to "hear" His still, small voice, but He is giving you pictures, you may push the pictures aside without recognizing that it is Him. If you feel like something is blocking you from hearing His voice, we encourage you to first be honest with yourself about anything that may be creating this block. Although it can be frustrating, it is necessary to identify the block. If you are still struggling to identify what is blocking you, you can also pray through the questions below. Once this has been addressed, we would encourage you to return to the previous question.

Pray: "Lord, I want to hear from you, but I am experiencing a block. Can You help identify anything that is blocking me receiving from You?" Write what He shows you below.

Ask: "God, what do You want me to do with the block that You have shown me?" Write what He shows you below.

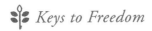

Keys to Freedom — Setting the Stage

Day 4: *Hearing the Voice of God – Part II*

As you have spent some time identifying how Jesus communicates with you as an individual, you may wonder how you are supposed to know if what you are receiving is actually from Him! Doubt can often come in and cause us to question the process and whether or not it is God speaking, especially when we are first learning to hear from Him.

If we call out to Him, what is God's promise to us in Jeremiah 33:3?

Throughout the Word, the Lord promises to speak to us, reveal Himself to us, and show us things that we "do not know." The Word of God tells us that He desires to communicate with us, but the Word also serves as a compass for everything that we receive from Him in prayer. As we discern whether or not what we receive is from the Lord, there are a few key ways that can help you to discern more clearly if you have heard or received something from Him.

It is confirmed in the Word. If what you receive does not line up with truth from the Bible, you will know that it is not from God. His voice and His Word always line up. For example, if you hear a voice telling you that you will marry a person who is already married, you know that is not God, because it does not line up with Scripture.

> *When the Lord communicates with us, His voice always brings hope, life, and love.*

It is confirmed by God's character. God is good, holy, just, and pure. If what you receive does not line up with His character, you will know that it is not from Him. When the Lord communicates with us, His voice always brings hope, life, and love. Even when God corrects us, He does it from a place of love and care, not guilt or condemnation (see Romans 8:1).

It is confirmed by the fruit it produces. Does the word you received produce the fruit of the Spirit (love, joy, peace, patience, kindness, goodness, faithfulness, gentleness, and self-control)? Or does it produce fear, discouragement, and confusion? If what you receive is from the Lord, it will always produce good fruit from the Spirit.

God will often speak to you through other means to confirm what He is saying. When you ask a Christian friend or pastor for wisdom, God often will use that person to affirm what He has told you. The Bible says, "By the testimony of two or three witnesses every word may be established" (Matt. 18:16). It is very helpful to seek out the wisdom and perspective of godly Christian leaders in your life when you are learning the ways you receive from the Lord and growing in your confidence in this area of your personal relationship with Him.

We encourage you to make a habit of asking Him to confirm to you whether or not the things you receive are from Him. God wants to speak to you more than you want Him to. As you make time and create space for Him to speak, He will be faithful to reveal Himself to you.

Below are a couple of questions to ask the Lord in prayer and space for you to write out His responses. (You can find more examples of these types of questions on the *Hearing the Voice of God* Freedom Tool at **www.MercyMultiplied.com/FreedomTools**).

"Father, what are two things that You see as good in me?"

"Lord, when You look into the future of my life, what is something You are excited about for me?"

We encourage you to read back over what you have received and written and simply thank the Lord for what He has shown you.

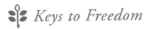

Day 5: *Stepping Forward*

This week has held a lot of information that we pray has become revelation as you have taken time with the Lord each day. As we wrap up this week's study on "Setting the Stage," we want to create space and time for you to process and think through what you have learned about the tree and hearing the voice of God. Identifying what we need to address and work on in our lives, and then inviting the Lord in to have a voice in that process, is what changes things and allows us to seek out healing and freedom from the root issues in our lives.

Take some time to prayerfully process the following questions:

What caused you to pick up / join this study?

What does freedom mean to you? If this is hard for you to define, perhaps take a moment and look up the definition in the dictionary.

Look back to the tree that you completed on Day 1. What are some of the branches of behavior that you would like to address during this study? How will you know when they have been addressed? What might change in you and your life due to this?

Setting the Stage — Keys to Freedom

Ask the Lord the following question in prayer: "Jesus, what is one thing that You desire for me to gain through this study? Is there any particular area that You desire for me to address and overcome?" Write what you receive in the space below.

As we wrap up this first full week, let's set our hearts to overcome the past and soar to places we've only dreamed of before. For some of you, it will be a significant departure from the life you live now. For others, it will seem more like a course correction. In every case, it will liberate you to be and do what you haven't been and done before. This path of freedom will impact your thoughts and emotions, your relationships with others, and your heart-to-heart connection with God. We encourage you to continue what you have started and to watch and see what He does in your life!

> *This path of freedom will impact your thoughts and emotions, your relationships with others, and your heart-to-heart connection with God.*

JOURNAL

What did God speak or show to you throughout the week?

Don't forget to share what God is doing in your life or any valuable insights you have received. And be sure to use the #KeystoFreedom hashtag!

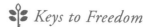

Key 1
Committing and Connecting to Christ

Deb's Story

Growing up, I was often told that I was an accident. I was a mistake. I heard the lies so often that I started to believe them. I remember making a deal with myself one night, that since I was a "bad girl", I was going to be the best bad girl that I could possibly be. I also experienced significant sexual abuse, which only fuelled my need for an escape from the pain. I started drinking, shoplifting and using drugs. I eventually got hooked on crystal meth.

A few years after high school, I headed for Hollywood, lured by the promise of big money and the seemingly glamorous lifestyle of the sex industry. For two decades, I slipped further and further into the sex industry, as my addiction to crystal meth grew stronger. I loved meth, because I could stay awake for weeks at a time, and there was a lot of partying going on that I didn't want to miss.

I never thought about getting help until the man I was seeing left me and broke my heart. I decided to go to rehab just to get away. I kept going back to rehab but I could never make it past 14 days. The flashbacks of things that had happened to me in my life were just so overwhelming that I actually welcomed back the relief that the drugs gave me.

One day a friend invited me to a Bible study (although she didn't tell me it was a Bible study!). I remember the leaders of the study singing a song with the lyrics: *Chains be broken, lives be healed, eyes be opened. Christ is revealed.* I started sobbing thinking to myself, "I have chains that need to be broken".

Those same ladies invited me to a Christian conference in Los Angeles called GodChicks. The founder of Mercy Multiplied, Nancy Alcorn, was a speaker at the event. Nancy started speaking about all kinds of issues and addictions and how people are told they can never change. I thought, "Yes, that's me. I keep being told I will never change."

But Nancy said something different: "That is not what the Word of God says! Second Corinthians 5:17 says, 'If any person be in Christ, they are a new creation. Old things have passed away, and all things are new!' The experts of the world inundate you with language like, 'Once an addict, always an addict.' That is absolutely not true. You have a choice. You can choose freedom!"

Nancy shared another scripture from Deuteronomy 30:19 that would forever change my life: "I set before you life and death, blessings and curses. Choose life." Nancy said that if anyone was there who had an eating disorder or drug or alcohol addiction, it did not matter! We could choose to be free!

And it hit me like a brick wall. I had never realized that I had a choice. In fact, I had been told that I would always be an addict, that I had a disease and that I would never change. I had been an addict for 30 years and was literally at the end of my rope. I so badly wanted to rid myself of the hell in which I lived. I was ready to choose life!

After the service, an usher took me up to Nancy. I was carrying a black bag that opened from the top, like an old-fashioned doctor's bag from house call days. It was full of drugs and drug paraphernalia.

I came up to Nancy with tears streaming down my face – tears of frustration, overwhelming emotions and even anger that I had never been told I had a choice. I said to her, "I am 42 years old and I've been doing drugs since I was 12. Are telling me that I can be free?"

Nancy looked me square in the eye and said emphatically, "Yes!"

I shoved my bag full of drug paraphernalia into Nancy's hands, threw my hands up in the air and said, "Pray for me. I don't want to be an addict anymore. I want freedom!"

Nancy was so happy that she literally began jumping for joy. She wanted to seize the moment because she knew God would meet me right where I was. Nancy prayed for that thirty-year addiction to be broken over my life. I handed over that black bag and fully surrendered to Jesus Christ that night.

I was 42 years old when I made that commitment and my life was never the same. People knew right away. I called people after the conference and they would respond, "What happened to you? You sound different." My voice was different. I was different. I still had to work through the pain from the sexual abuse and the root issues of the drug addiction, but through the mercy and grace of Jesus, the addiction itself left me that night. That was exactly 3,341 days ago (as of the time of this writing), and I have lived drug-free ever since. And now that I am clean from drugs, instead of hiding from the world in fear of my next relapse, I have the power, love and sound mind of Jesus! I am truly a new creation in Christ!

Key 1: Committing and Connecting to Christ 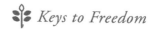 Keys to Freedom

Day 1: *From the Inside Out*

Changing our lives and living in freedom and wholeness is an inside job. Yet we are so often caught up with the external things of life and whether or not we look like we have it all together.

In Jesus' day the religious leaders were the ones who tried to hold it all together. Their clothes were meticulously cleaned, their hands washed down to a science, and their prayers seemingly pious. But Jesus shocked them by calling them "whitewashed tombs" full of dead men's bones (Matt. 23:27). That's a pretty strong rebuke!

Jesus sees reality inside and out. He knew those men were not being transformed from the inside out by God's living presence. The warnings He gave them are for us as well. You and I may look good on the outside, but are we subconsciously covering up the real issues and hurts on the inside? Jesus may have sounded harsh, but He was not condemning those religious leaders. He was offering them freedom. He does the same with us.

Imagine having a kettle that is plugged into the power source, but the power switch is turned off. It looks like a kettle and has the potential to boil like a kettle, but until it is switched on, it is of no use and cannot fulfill its potential! We can look like Christians by going to church and Bible studies, but if our lives are disconnected from the power source, if we are not vitally united to Christ, we risk missing the truth, power, and freedom that Jesus died for us to have.

> *We can look like Christians by going to church and Bible studies, but if our lives are disconnected from the power source, if we are not vitally united to Christ, we risk missing the truth, power and freedom that Jesus died for us to have.*

If you want to be free – really free – you need to come to a place of complete surrender and commitment to the Freedom Giver, Jesus Christ. You need to connect (perhaps for the first time) to the power source for living life in freedom and wholeness.

Before we move on, if you have not committed your life to Christ, now is the perfect opportunity! This entire study was written with the idea that the reader has committed his or her life to Christ. Consider carefully and deeply the total commitment it requires. If you have never given your heart to Him, or you have, but now know that you've held much of it back and relied on your own coping mechanisms, then we invite you to commit or reconnect to the One who holds it all – your past, your present, your future. This study will not set you free; only Jesus can do that.

If you would like to know more about what it truly means to commit your life to Christ, we must start by having a right perspective of who God really is. He is eternal. He is the Creator and Owner of all things. He is the one and only God who is worthy of all the worship of everything that exists.

However, starting in the Garden of Eden, mankind turned and worshipped the things that God made instead of worshipping the One who made them. (Read Genesis 3 if you don't know the story). Ever since then, mankind has continued to commit this sin. The Bible tells us in Romans 3:12 that "All have turned away … there is no one who does good, not even one." We all have fallen short and given our hearts to sin and to the worship of other things. In doing so, we have turned our hearts away from Him. We are all guilty.

How does God respond to our turning away? He is perfectly just and perfectly holy (set apart). As such, God and sin cannot coexist. So, His first response to our sin is separation from Him in a place called Hell. Hell is described in the Bible as a place of everlasting torment and punishment. It is where we are all destined to spend eternity because we are all guilty of sin. We are desperate to be rescued.

Thankfully, God has a second response to sin. He is not only perfectly just and holy; He is also perfectly loving and merciful. The second response is Jesus. God sent His Son to the world to live a perfect life and, at the appointed time, go to the cross. It was at the cross that God poured out His wrath against mankind on Jesus.

What does 2 Corinthians 5:21 say? Write it in the space below.

God chose to make Jesus, who knew no sin, to be sin for us! Then God raised Jesus from the dead after three days and conquered the enemy on our behalf. Because of Jesus, we have the chance to no longer be enemies of God. We have right standing before Him because of the cross. Our final destination no longer has to be Hell; it can be life with Him!

Jesus paid for our sins when He went to the cross. He is our only hope. All that He has asked you to do is confess your sins to Him and receive the gift of salvation.

Key 1: Committing and Connecting to Christ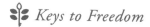

Write Romans 10:10, 13 below. What is required of us to be saved?

The invitation to give your life to Jesus is coming from Jesus Himself! If you desire to give your life to Him and place your faith in the cross of Christ, tell Him right now. How exciting that you want to become a follower of Jesus! It is the hands-down greatest and most important decision you will ever make!

If that is the desire and decision of your heart, we encourage you to find a Bible-based church in your community (or an older mentor or friend who you know is a Christian and can connect you with a church). Tell that person about your desire to give your life to Jesus and follow Him. We pray that you would find a church that will celebrate with you, guide you, and help you walk out this awesome decision. Congratulations!

Day 2: *All In*

Deb's story at the beginning of this week is the story of a woman who, for many years, relied on something other than Jesus to keep her life upright. Drugs were her way of coping with the challenges of life and the pain of her past. They gave her a sense of support and comfort, even though they were destructive to her body, mind, and soul.

We all have the need to feel a sense of belonging, acceptance, and significance, but if we find those things outside of a fully committed relationship with Jesus, there will come a point when those stabilizers are just too restrictive. Like a small child who has learned how to ride a bike with training wheels, it may feel and look as if you're riding the bike of your life, but there comes a point when those training wheels are the very things that become more of a hindrance than a support. Those artificial stabilizers that once made you feel balanced now hold you back, restrict your speed, and prevent you from being able to explore the fullness of freedom that a total commitment to Jesus has to offer.

God is asking for us to trust Him by letting go of every artificial stabilizer and every self-generated coping or defense mechanism we have used to respond to life's challenges. If we let Him, He will teach us the wonder of learning to ride the bike of our lives without the restriction of training wheels. He will teach us to ride in freedom, but it requires us giving Him our total commitment.

Write a brief synopsis of the story in Matthew 19:16-26 in the space below.

To relate it to the bike analogy, the young man in this story could have been saying, "How do I ride a big bike? I can see the life you are talking about, Jesus, and I want it. I want to follow you, to ride alongside you, but my bike doesn't seem to be able to." Jesus' response would be something along the lines of, "Okay, let me show you the basics – backside on seat, hands on handle bars, feet on pedals, now go!" And the man says, "I've done all of that, so what's left?" Clearly the man knows he's missing something. He can feel a restriction on him, but he can't work out what it is. Maybe you feel the same way. You want to live free from whatever is holding you back, and you've done all the basics - you've given your life to Him; you're going to church; you're reading your Bible and praying; yet, something's still not quite right.

But then Jesus pinpoints the artificial stabilizer that was keeping the rich man's life upright and moving forward in his own strength. His security, identity, sense of power, worth, and value were all tied up in his riches. Jesus asks him to let go, to sell his stuff, to take off the artificial stabilizers, and learn to ride the bike of his life by trusting Him.

Maybe for you it's not money; maybe it's a relationship, an addiction, or your job, title or position. Whatever it is, if you are trying to follow Jesus and desire to know the fullness and the freedom of the open road with no restrictions, then you've got to learn to take off the training wheels! Give Jesus your whole heart and all that is keeping you artificially upright. It is the only way to fully connect with Him and experience true freedom.

Deb's past life was in that black bag—and she gave it all up. Imagine the comfort and familiarity of the drugs and drug paraphernalia that had defined her existence for thirty years. Think of the objects she was used to handling every day, the routine she followed, the people she interacted with, and the daily rhythm of her life. Each of us has a "black bag" full of old, familiar stuff that tries to get in the way of our connection with Him. Would you have the courage to make such a sudden break when you saw that freedom was possible on the other side of your choice? Would you push it all away in a moment?

When God reveals to you that something is getting in the way of your commitment and relationship with Him, it's time to let it go. Not some of it – all of it. God has given you a choice between life and death, captivity and freedom. He will honor your choice either way. The truth is that the amount of "death" operating in your life right now is potentially linked to your level of connection to Christ. Are you all in for God? Or are you holding back? It takes humility to admit when we're partially committed to God, but if you have an area you want to overcome, you're going to need His grace to do so.

> *God has given you a choice between life and death, captivity and freedom.*

Do you believe God has your complete and total commitment? If not, ask the Lord to show you the biggest hindrance(s) in your life that are keeping you from total commitment.

What would it take for you to give your "old black bag" of stuff – your artificial stabilizers – to God and walk away from it? Of all the things in that bag, what would be the most difficult to surrender to Him? Why?

Now that you have identified some areas that are holding you back, you have the choice to hand those to the Lord in an act of surrender. Surrender is one of the most powerful postures that we can take before the Lord. Surrender positions us for the fullness and freedom that He desires to give. Surrender is a posture of the heart, but it can also be a posture of our physical body. If you choose to pray through the prayer included below, and are willing and able, we would encourage you to posture your physical body in a position of surrender as well. This may mean getting down on your knees or another physical position that mirrors the surrender in your heart. When you are ready, you can pray this surrender prayer to the Lord:

> *Father, I desire to be all in when it comes to my relationship with You. I recognize that there are some areas of my life that I have held back from You and have not fully surrendered or trusted You to take care of. I choose right now, in the Name of Jesus, to surrender _____ (list areas here) to You. I don't want anything to hold me back or serve as an artificial stabilizer in my life. I lay each of these things in Your hands, and thank You for caring so deeply about the things, people, and relationships that are important to me. In this moment, I fully surrender these areas, my life, and my heart to You in Jesus' Name, Amen.*

Day 3: *The Traps – Part I*

Those who have a difficult time giving their total commitment to Christ often fall into a few deadly traps, and we're going to take a look at some of those traps over the next couple of days.

Trap #1: "I Tried God, and It Didn't Work for Me."

Sometimes when people commit their life to Christ, they want to see big changes in all areas of their lives immediately. Big changes do happen, but many changes take time. Many times God's blueprint in dealing with His children is a process. We can see an example of God's blueprint by the way He chose to create the heavens and the earth. God chose to create the universe over the course of seven days. This means He intentionally chose to create everything in existence using process. Think about it. God is all-powerful. He could have easily spoken creation into immediate existence with one all-encompassing word, but He didn't. He embraced the process, took His time, and allowed the very essence of process to be weaved into the very essence of our existence.

Everywhere we look there is process, but so often, we resent it or try to avoid it by finding shortcuts to our destination. We are increasingly surrounded by quick fix, instant results, and same-day delivery solutions to whatever our problem is. We want the end result but are often not prepared to do what it takes to get there. We want the victory but not the battle, the fitness but not the training. It's not often that we get one without the other.

Maybe you are facing a mountain of debt or have suffered the death of a loved one, and the grief seems insurmountable. Maybe your children are far from God, or you have had your heart broken and desperately want to move forward, but you don't know how. Whatever it may be, the likelihood is that your breakthrough, your miracle, will not be a one-time event; it will be a process.

Even doing this study is not your ultimate breakthrough. This study is not a formula or a magic wand that sets you free. It will teach you the principles of freedom and wholeness, but actually putting them into practice is a process that will extend way beyond these few weeks that we share together.

What is Jesus called in Hebrews 12:2? What does that tell you about His role?

God's job is to address and perfect the things that are important to you. Your first step of faith may be simply to rest in Him and choose to trust that He has everything under control. He started the relationship, and He's in the lead.

Process is how God builds us up. Process is often His way of growing us, maturing us, and drawing us closer into relationship with Him. But thankfully, God does not abandon us to this process. He does not place Himself at the final destination point, impatiently awaiting our arrival and scolding us for our tardiness. Instead, He lovingly and graciously walks alongside us. He enters into the discomfort of the journey and provides the comfort we so desperately need along the way.

> *Process is how God builds us up. It's His way of growing us, maturing us and drawing us closer into relationship with Him.*

He speaks encouragement, direction, and gives us the grace we need to carry on. His presence can combat the fear we feel, the uncertainty we sense, and provide the strength we lack. That is the miracle. The God of Heaven and Earth extends His hand to each of us and says, "It's time to go, time to change, time to grow, time to face your giants – and I will help you."

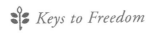

Read Philippians 1:6 and ask, "Holy Spirit, why is it important for me to understand and believe this scripture in my life?" Write down what He shares with you in the space below.

Day 4: *The Traps – Part II*

Trap #2: "I Need to Clean Up My Life."

When we surrender our lives to Christ, we receive the most amazing exchange. Jesus takes our sin and old life and gives us His righteousness (2 Cor. 5:21). You won't find a better exchange than that. He gives you the opportunity to experience a life of healing and wholeness now. He also gives you eternal life with Him, and we didn't do a thing to deserve it!

For some people, that's the obstacle. They find it hard to accept God's gift as free. It's so opposite of the human system, which gives us only what we earn and deserve.

If any of the following statements describe your viewpoint, you may have a hard time making that total commitment. Put a check mark next to any you relate to.

___ I'll accept God's gift of salvation, but there are some areas I want to clean up first.
___ I don't really deserve God's mercy.
___ I don't want to fully commit because I know I won't be able to do it perfectly.

These statements are lies. Jesus' message is, "Come as you are" (John 7:37; Luke 18:13).

Key 1: Committing and Connecting to Christ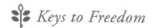

Many Christians have a hard time switching gears from their worldly mentality and accepting that Jesus welcomes them even though they are not good enough. It can be hard to rest on His goodness and not our own. It can be a challenge to understand why He would take all our mistakes and declare us "not guilty" before the Father. Jesus stands next to us with pride and joy before God, and we appear pure and clean – without earning a bit of it.

Maybe the judgment of God is a lot easier to accept than His mercy. Judgment makes sense to us; mercy doesn't. Judgment fits into our human logic. It can take some time to love mercy as much as we love judgment. When we do, we are liberated at a deep level. We find rest in Jesus. God has chosen to show mercy to people. We don't have a choice in the matter. We will never be good enough to deserve it. The only thing you can do is let go of your pride and say, "Yes!"

Trap #3: "I Will Always Have My Problem Even If I Follow Jesus."

It is common in society for people to believe that anyone with problems will always have those struggles. The phrase, "Once an addict, always an addict" is commonly heard even in Christian circles. In fact, many treatment programs and psychiatric wards use the terms "recovering addict," "recovering alcoholic," and "recovering from depression." Through our experience with young women at Mercy, we have seen this terminology to be problematic, because it keeps someone tied to their past and continually identifying with the very area from which they have received freedom!

At Mercy, we are not about treatment; we are about transformation. The Bible teaches us in 2 Corinthians 5:17 that if anyone receives Christ, that person is "a new creation; old things have passed away; behold, all things have become new" (NKJV). The old person we used to be is dead and gone at salvation, and we now start a new life with a new beginning, no longer identifying with our past. We are all aware that we have a past, but we do not have to identify with our past and allow our past to destroy our future. We can move forward in our new identity as children of God – forgiven and free!

> *We do not have to allow our past to destroy our future.*

Have you ever been told or believed that you will never overcome a certain area in your life? What feelings and thoughts did that cause in you?

Study Guide | 37

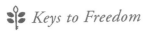

Does it make a difference for you to know that freedom is actually possible? If so, how?

Take a look back over the three traps discussed yesterday and today. Do you believe that any of the traps apply to you? If so, which one(s)?

Let's end today by making a prayer of total commitment to Jesus. He has a purpose and plan for you that will completely amaze you, and it starts with the choice to fully commit and connect with Him each day. Let's pray:

Lord, I love You. No one has ever done more good for me than You, and no one ever will. You deserve my total trust and commitment, and with a sincere heart, I offer it to You now. Help me to lay that strong foundation and to walk in the freedom and benefits of a total commitment to You. Thank You for totally committing to me when you chose to lay down Your life in the hope of having a relationship with me one day. I fully commit to our relationship now and look forward to all that is ahead. In Jesus' Name, Amen.

Now that we have fully committed our lives and connected our hearts to Jesus, it's important to discuss another area of great blessing that is ours – our authority in Christ. We will begin this discussion tomorrow.

Key 1: Committing and Connecting to Christ  Keys to Freedom

Day 5: *Authority in Christ*

We have discussed the importance of choosing to commit and connect to Christ, so now we can move toward understanding our authority as believers.

The importance of understanding our authority as a believer is an essential part of living free and staying free! We live in a fallen world – a territory currently ruled by an enemy. As Christ-followers, we have been tasked with bringing Heaven's rule and reign to earth. In other words, we are called and created to operate within our rights, responsibilities, and authority as sons and daughters of the King, not as slaves to an enemy dictator who rules with fear and shame. We were created for freedom!

As we begin this discussion, it's important that we understand what "authority" actually means. One definition of authority is "delegated power." So the value of our authority rests on the power that is behind it. This is really great news because the God of the universe is the power behind our authority as believers. And when we understand this and know how to exercise that authority, we can face the enemy fearlessly!

What does 1 John 3:8 say about why Jesus came to Earth?

The cross is where Satan was defeated. When Jesus died on the cross, it seemed like Satan was victorious over Him. But on the third day, Jesus rose from the grave and, therefore, triumphed over the enemy! In that moment, Satan was stripped of his authority. In fact, before Jesus went back to heaven, He actually said in Matthew 28:18, "All authority in heaven and on earth has been given to me." Then, Christ chose to give that authority to us, so Christ's victory over the enemy is our victory when we are His!

Our battles with the enemy should always be with the consciousness that we have authority over him through Christ because he is a defeated foe. Jesus defeated him for us. And when we are born again, we receive this authority! We inherit the Name of Jesus, which is above every name, and now we can use that Name against the enemy!

> *Our battles with the enemy should always be with the consciousness that we have authority over him through Christ, because he is a defeated foe.*

Study Guide | 39

Key 1: Committing and Connecting to Christ

Write the following Scriptures in your own words.

1 John 4:4

James 4:7

The importance of understanding our authority is foundational to this entire study and our lives as believers in Christ. Imagine you have a $20 bill stuck in a pocket in a pair of pants, but you don't know it's there. Because you are unaware of it, you won't use it, and it won't do you any good. This is similar to our authority. If we don't know that we have it, we won't use it, and can therefore unknowingly walk around in bondage!

Knowing your authority in Christ allows you to stand firm against the enemy, and it will also radically change the way you pray. When you understand your authority, you begin to understand that through prayer, you can make a declaration that whatever the Lord has promised to you in His Word is yours!

When you make a decree over your life, you demand your rights as a son or daughter of God. And to be clear, you're not demanding of God when you demand your rights; you're demanding of the enemy what is yours because God has promised it to you, and you have the authority to lay claim to it!

Job 22:28 says, "You will declare a thing, and it will be established for you; so light will shine on your ways (NKJV)." The Word encourages us not to just pray, but to declare and decree the promises of God over our lives.

Key 1: Committing and Connecting to Christ

Keys to Freedom

What decrees (not just prayers) could you begin to declare over your life in order to demand from the enemy what is yours? (If you need ideas, reference the declarations in Appendix C.) We also encourage you to ask the Lord what He would have you declare. Write some of your decrees below.

It's so important for you to know your inheritance as a son or daughter of God. It's FREEDOM. It's HEALING. It's FORGIVENESS. It's LOVE. It's JOY. It's PEACE. And you get to lay claim to those promises. You get to claim your inheritance. The enemy knows that he cannot hold in bondage a believer who knows their authority in Christ. As we move through the keys to freedom over the coming weeks, let's do it from a position of authority over our enemy!

 *Keys to Freedom*   Key 1: Committing and Connecting to Christ

JOURNAL

What did God speak or show to you throughout the week?

Don't forget to share what God is doing in your life or any valuable insights you have received.
And be sure to use the #KeystoFreedom hashtag!

Key 2
Renewing Your Mind

Julie's Story

I have spent so many years of my life feeling imprisoned by thoughts that do not agree with God's truth about me. Thoughts like… "I don't fit in. People don't like me. I am stupid." These thoughts were based on circumstances in my life where I had failed. I then allowed those experiences to determine my beliefs about myself. Those thoughts did not feel like lies. To me, they were the truth, so I found ways to cover up what I thought were shameful truths about myself.

"I am stupid" was a particular battle for me. Despite being given a very privileged college education at one of the best private schools in the country, I did not thrive under the pressure of exams. The more I tried to do well, the worse I seemed to do! I had no idea what I wanted to major in, so I decided to look into teaching children. This degree required me to take some math courses. I spent four years studying, and I failed eight exams during that time, which only furthered the belief that I was stupid and did not have what it takes to be successful. I spent my final year in college giving every hour I could to study, determined to do well. I graduated with a degree in Math, but with a grade of which I was not proud and saw no reason to celebrate.

I spent years living under a lie that I was not good enough and did not have what it takes to succeed. As a result, I became afraid of failure, of getting it wrong, and of embarrassing myself. I eventually ended up in an accounting position, in part because I knew that my math degree would get me the job, but with little faith that I would perform well. Despite promotions and success, I still felt stupid.

While taking a leadership class, I reached the end of myself during one particular writing assignment. I didn't want to continue, as I couldn't bear the thought of experiencing failure all over again. I remember choosing to continue with the writing assignment from a new belief: I purposefully trusted that I was wise, and I believed I did have something good to say. I wrote the assignment in my own way, not fulfilling the requirements I thought were the expectation. I submitted it and received the highest grade you could for a piece of work. I was amazed!

All this time, I had tried to do what I thought people wanted me to do and failed. When I came into agreement with the Truth, I flourished! I found myself repenting of the lie that I was stupid, and in that moment, I heard God whisper to me, "You thought I had given you one of the worst brains, but I have given you one of the best." I had lived under the lid of comparison, shame, failure, and rejection for all those years. But when I made the choice to be myself and start believing the things that God said about me, freedom was unlocked in a moment. This moment was hugely significant, but it was just a start! I had to commit to a process of identifying each lie I believed that didn't line up with what God thought about me and start actively renewing my mind.

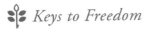 *Keys to Freedom*   Key 2: Renewing Your Mind

Day 1: *Higher Thoughts*

The Word of God says that when we renew our minds our lives will be changed: "Don't copy the behavior and customs of this world, but let God transform you into a new person by changing the way you think" (Rom. 12:2, NLT). Renewing your mind means to do away with unhealthy thought patterns and to replace them with true, godly ones. It is impossible to do without God's help.

> *The only way to re-direct our thoughts is to stop walking down the old thought trails and choose to create new ones that take us in a different direction.*

Formed in our early childhood years, our thought patterns and belief system inform us on how we view the world around us, relationships, and ourselves. In many ways, our thought patterns act like hiking trails. Constructing a trail requires some short-term effort of removing trees and creating a tread surface. But how are trails maintained? Simply by people regularly walking on them, right? The more a trail is traversed, the more established it becomes. On the other hand, if people cease to walk on the trail, it will eventually disappear.

In a similar way, our thoughts often follow neurological pathways without a conscious decision from us, and just like a hiking trail, our thoughts will lead us to the same destination each time. These thought trails have been well used over the years and many of them developed from a young age. The only way to re-direct our thoughts is to stop walking down the old thought trails and choose to create new ones that take us in a different direction. Breaking down the old well-worn trails of thought doesn't happen involuntarily. A characteristic of our brain called "neuroplasticity" enables us to actually change the way our brains work. Rather than always replaying the old negative thoughts, you can introduce new true thoughts into your mind. Over time, these thoughts will actually become more common and natural in your mind than the old faulty beliefs. This is the process the Bible calls "renewing the mind." Science has proven that it is possible to completely redirect our neurological pathways.

It's important for us to recognize that when it comes to our thoughts, we can choose between God's truth and light or the enemy's lies and darkness. We will experience great freedom when we allow God's light to lead our thoughts.

Can you identify areas of your thought life that are often led by the lies of the enemy? Is this something you would like to change by surrendering your thought life to God and His truth? Explain your answer.

In the first full week of study, we discussed the tree analogy. Let's discuss an example of how our roots, belief systems, and behaviors are all connected, so that we can be more clearly see the significance of the process of renewing our minds.

Let's say that a behavior you struggle with is people pleasing. Maybe you find it difficult to say "no" to requests from people, especially people who you admire or respect, like a boss, pastor, or spouse. This means you are always serving, always working overtime, always saying "yes" to the detriment of your health or your family or your own needs. Your sense of value and worth becomes driven by a constant need to perform and gain approval from others. Every mistake and perceived criticism takes you a long time to get over, but any compliments given only last a short moment in their "feel good" factor.

The thought patterns (belief system) upholding these behaviors could be:
- "People will love and accept me only if I work hard to please them and do everything right."
- "No matter how hard I work, I will always fall short. Nothing I do will ever be good enough."
- "I must earn love and approval."

The root causes related to this belief system could be:
- Rejection
- Fear (especially of failure)
- Pride

The life experiences where these roots were formed could be:
- Workaholic parents (especially if they are high achievers)
- High-pressured school environment
- History of being bullied
- Over-achieving siblings
- Always being rewarded for performance, not for character

Hopefully, this example gives you a clearer understanding of how the "tree trunk" of our thought life is connected to the roots and our behaviors. We all have a belief system with thought patterns that have grown out from the roots and connect to our behaviors. Tomorrow we are going to start taking a closer look at the thought patterns and belief system at work in our own lives so that we can begin addressing them head-on!

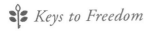 Keys to Freedom   Key 2: Renewing Your Mind

Day 2: *Thinking is a Choice*

Some people think it is God's job to renew our minds and that our job is to sit passively by and let it happen without exerting any effort. Arianna Walker, Executive Director of Mercy UK, tells of a dream she had during a difficult time in her life. This God-given dream helped her to understand the importance of being responsible for what goes on inside our own minds instead of assuming that God will do it all for us.

Just before she went to bed one night, Arianna was reading Psalm 23:5: "You prepare a banquet before me in the presence of my enemies." In a dream that night, Arianna saw herself sitting at a large round dining table in a restaurant. Around the table were her guests: Faith, Hope, Love, Joy, Peace, Wisdom, and Strength. They chatted, laughed, and sang together like the good friends they were. The scene was one of joy, fellowship, and friendship.

As Arianna watched the scene in her dream, she became aware of three figures that stood over in the shadows beside the bar. Wondering who they were, she felt God tell her that they were her enemies: Fear, Worry, and Unbelief. These enemies stared at her with such hatred that it sent a cold ripple through her body. She asked God, "Why are they here? They don't belong in this place." And He answered, "This restaurant, like your life, is open to the public. Life on earth is an open space that can sometimes be visited by enemies. But who sits at your table is by invitation only." Even in her dream, the truth of that statement hit her like a ton of bricks.

As she continued to observe the scene, she saw herself become distracted by the figures at the bar. Each time she would steal a glance in their direction or cease the conversation with her companions, she could see them move towards her. Finally, Fear stood directly behind the seat of Faith, and the entire scene stopped still. Everyone went quiet. The tension was palpable in the air, as both Fear and Faith looked her directly in the eyes. And then she heard the voice of God, "There are no more seats at your table and Faith will not share her seat with Fear. Choose your companions wisely."

> *We cannot always control what thoughts walk through the door of our minds, but we can choose which thoughts we allow to "sit out our table".*

Arianna woke up and realized the battles she faced would be won or lost in her mind and in her thoughts. Our external world will always be open to the presence of our enemies, but we decide what gets to sit down at the table of our thoughts.

Many times, due to past trauma or lies planted by the enemy, thoughts may enter our minds that we did not intentionally think on our own. This is a new concept to many people, and it's an important one. Thoughts will come to us uninvited, and we cannot always control

Key 2: Renewing Your Mind

what thoughts walk through the door of our minds, but we can choose which thoughts we allow to "sit at our table." Once that thought or memory enters our mind, we can either focus on it, or make the choice to kick it out and renew our minds.

Often, at this point in the discussion, our emotions can start to rise up and disagree. If you have lived a life in which your emotions have controlled your thought life, do not be surprised if you have some work to do to put your will before your emotions. If your emotions don't agree with the Word of God, they are speaking lies to you. Choosing to renew your mind and stand on truth is not about how you feel; it is by faith. Inside of you is a faith muscle. Just like any muscle, it takes time and practice to isolate it, flex it, and feel it working. Soon, you realize you're gaining strength. Your feelings and emotions will take notice and allow your will to take the lead. Your desires, attractions, and opinions will also begin to change and line up with truth. This is why the Bible says so clearly for us to take an active role in choosing our thoughts.

Write out 2 Corinthians 10:5 in your own words. What does this scripture say about your choice regarding your thought life?

How can you begin to take ownership over your thoughts?

Is there anyone sitting at the "table" of your thought life who needs to have their invitation revoked? Who? Who should take their place at the table?

Keys to Freedom

Key 2: Renewing Your Mind

What does Philippians 4:8 tell us to think about?

As you focus on the things listed in Philippians 4:8 and the truth of the Word, you will find that there is less space and opportunity for the lies, negative thoughts, and difficult memories to pop up in your mind.

Day 3: *Meditating on the Truth*

We discussed yesterday that nothing gets to sit down at the table of our thoughts apart from an invitation from us. We actually have the ability to decide what we will do with our thoughts. And deciding to invite God's truth to sit down at our table will bring amazing peace, clarity and freedom to our lives!

What will be the result of knowing God's Truth according to the following scriptures?

Psalm 119:105

John 8:31–32

Jesus tells us in John 8:32 that the truth will set you free. This is a commonly quoted scripture but often without context. Jesus actually says: "And you shall *know* the truth and the truth will set you free."

> *It's not simply the truth that sets you free; it's the truth you know that sets you free.*

Therefore, it's not simply the truth that sets you free; it's the truth you know that sets you free. And how else will you know the truth than to read the source of truth – the Word of God? Being able to respond to the trials and adversity of life from a godly perspective means we need to develop a love for God's Word, during good times and bad.

Key 2: Renewing Your Mind 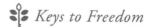 Keys to Freedom

His promises, His belief in us, His character, and His plans and purposes for our lives are found within the books of the Bible. Knowing and believing these qualities of God are essential to giving us the ability to turn simple words on a page to life-giving freedom.

When we meditate on the Word and choose what we think about, we are empowered to take a much more active role in renewing our minds. God never promised that no weapon will be formed against us, but that no weapon formed against us will prosper (Isa. 54:17). When we latch on to His truth, the weapons—the lies, fears, and hurts—will not prosper. We learn to actively break agreement with the lies we have believed and begin to stand on the power of His truth.

What does Psalm 1:1-2 say about the man that meditates on the Word of God?

What do you think it means to meditate on God's Word? How will it help?

Imagine if you were to spill liquid on the floor, and you had two options for mopping it up – newspaper or a paper towel. While the newspaper may be similar in composition to the paper towel, it only has a limited ability to absorb the liquid. It won't clean up the spill. The paper towel, on the other hand, absorbs every ounce of liquid and carries it within itself. Learning to absorb the Word of God into the very core of what we believe about ourselves, about Him, and about life is the very essence of what it means to renew our minds. It is how we come to know the truth, and knowing that truth is what sets us free. The lie has no power over you unless you believe it. But the same is true for the truth; it has no power to change you unless you choose to believe it and put it to work in your life.

By putting the Word of God to work in our lives, we experience freedom, healing, and restoration. Light dispels the darkness. As the light of God's Word goes into your mind, it pushes the darkness out. Then the freedom of Christ begins to connect to your heart in a deeper way. The key is to immerse ourselves in the Word. It says, "Faith comes by hearing, and hearing by the word of God" (Rom. 10:17, NKJV). We need to hear God's Word over and over again to remind ourselves of who we are in Christ. We need to speak it to ourselves with our mouths so our own ears hear our voice saying the truth.

Living in freedom and renewing your mind means hiding God's Word in your heart with regular, passionate meditation and memorization. As you do, you will begin to forge a new, clear, and trustworthy trail in your mind that will continue to be easier and easier to walk and enjoy.

Are you currently immersing yourself in Scripture through study, meditation, and memorization? If not, what are some things you could do to make space in your life for more of God's Word?

We want to encourage you to choose one of the things you listed in the last question and commit to put that thing to work this week and see what fruit comes from it.

The Word of God is our powerful weapon to defeat the enemy. When Jesus was tempted after fasting forty days, even He, the sinless, spotless Lamb of God, answered the enemy's temptations with, "It is written" (Matt. 4:4). If Jesus had to do that, how much more do we need to do it? Make "It is written" a regular part of your internal conversation and thought life. It works against all kinds of temptation and lies. Proverbs 3:5–6 is a well-known verse and tells us, "Trust in the Lord with all your heart and lean not on your own understanding." When we don't renew our minds, we naturally lean on our own understanding because that's all there is for us. But if you renew your mind to God's Word and His ways, you will walk in more and more freedom day-by-day, moment-by-moment.

Day 4: *Securing Our Weapons*

Over the next couple of days, we are going to talk about some practical ways to renew your mind with the Word of God. This will be very interactive and will take some work, so set aside a decent amount of time for today and tomorrow's study. It's too important to rush! We pray that this tool will be something you use for the rest of your life.

> *Our actions begin with our thought lives, so behind every negative habit or area of bondage is a lie.*

As the truth of the Word becomes the focus of our thought life, we can begin to address the lies that keep us stuck. Renewing our minds starts with understanding some of the lies we think and believe. Our actions begin with our thought lives, so behind every negative habit or area of bondage is a lie. One way to identify a belief system or thought pathway we have is to pay attention to what plays over and over in our minds and what comes out of our mouths. The Bible tells us that out of the overflow of the heart, the mouth speaks (Luke 6:45). So if we want to identify our belief system, sometimes we just need to pay attention to our own words.

- "It's not that big a deal. It helps me get through the day."
- "I'm ugly and worthless."
- "I have to promote myself. Nobody else will do it for me."
- "All authority is bad. I cannot trust someone who is in authority over me."
- "Depression is just part of who I am. I'm a melancholy person."
- "With the way I look, nobody could love me."
- "Given what happened to me in the past, I'm damaged goods."
- "God expects me to take care of myself. He only steps in when something is too big for me to handle."
- "I was always told to be seen and not heard, so I prefer to stay silent."

Thoughts like these do not measure up to the truth of God's Word. The tool of renewing our minds is God's way of helping us to break free from the destructive destination of our old hiking trails and help us to re-direct the trails of our thoughts in the direction of His truth.

What are some of the common phrases you say or think about yourself? List them in the space below.

We play untrue thoughts through our heads so frequently that we effectively memorize them and convince ourselves that they are true. We write the scripts of our own lives based on lies supplied by the enemy and difficult circumstances that we experience. As we mentioned on the first day of this week, science tells us that repetitive thoughts become physical "trails" in the brain that affect our reasoning, choices, and eventually, our beliefs. The problem is that once those trails are well worn in our minds and we are convinced that our thoughts are true, it becomes more and more difficult to recognize them for the lies that they are.

Based off the thoughts that you listed in the last question, ask the Lord to highlight one specific lie that has power in your life, and that He wants you to focus on for today and tomorrow's lesson. Write what He reveals to you in the space below.

The young women at Mercy find freedom from lies in a very practical way that every believer can use: They write out scriptures and "truth statements" on index cards and read them out loud. We need to hear ourselves speak the truth out loud to counter the lies that are working to gain access to our minds and, eventually, our hearts.

For example, one of our residents was really struggling with feelings of social anxiety because she believed the lie that people judged her in social settings. When feeling anxious, she would read the card that said, "I have the mind of Christ, and He gives me peace." It pushed out the lie of anxiety and enabled her to step into the peace Jesus makes available.

Many people believe the lie that God abandoned them when they needed Him the most. But the truth is that "God is our refuge and strength, an ever-present help in trouble" (Ps. 46:1). We can say with confidence, "I will fear no evil; for you are with me; your rod and your staff, they comfort me" (Ps. 23:4).

Today, you are going to start building your own collection of scripture cards to read from to renew your mind!

Grab at least five index cards, and start digging through the Bible to find truth to replace the lie that the Lord just highlighted to you above. When you come across a scripture or truth statement that really resonates with your heart in relation to that specific lie, write it on an index card. (You will want to write one scripture per index card.)

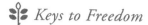

It may feel overwhelming for you to try to find applicable verses, so here are a few tips:
- Search for key words in the concordance section of your Bible (typically in the back), or use a topical Bible to search for scriptures by topic.
- Refer to Appendices A and B at the back of this book for scriptural truths.
- Read Ephesians 1 and 2 and/or Psalm 139. Those passages of Scripture are full of truths for renewing the mind.

We would also encourage you to be in prayer as you look through the Word, asking the Holy Spirit to highlight scriptures, as well as His thoughts and His heart towards you.

You may choose to do more than five scripture cards today if you like. However, we pray this will be a practice that you continue to use throughout the course of this study and for the rest of your life! Once you have identified the lie and you have identified what God's truth is regarding that lie, it's time to actually engage in the process of replacing the lie with that truth. Tomorrow's activity will focus on this process.

Day 5: *Steps to Renewing Your Mind*

We are going to spend today walking through how to summarize, personalize, and vocalize the Word of God, specifically as it relates to the lie you are currently addressing. Here is an explanation of each step:

Summarize It

When the Lord highlights a specific scripture to you, take some time to summarize it in your own words. This will cause you to draw out the meaning in a comprehensive way, considering every aspect of it. By putting it in your own words, you will process the meaning and digest it more fully.

> **Go through each of the scripture cards you wrote yesterday. On the back of each card write a summary of the meaning of that scripture in your own words. (Leave some space on each card for the next step.)**

Personalize It

Next, ask God what He is saying to you personally through the scripture so you can speak it out loud. The Holy Spirit speaks to us through the Word, illuminating certain truths specifically for us at just the right time. How many times have you read a verse that you have read many times before, only to find that this time it jumps off the page and virtually glows with life and meaning? That is the Holy Spirit personalizing the scripture to your immediate circumstance. Pay attention to those moments, and meditate on those verses of Scripture. Give Him time to speak to you about how they relate to your situation.

Go through each of your scripture cards, and ask God what the verses mean for you now. Ask Him in what ways you can put them to work in your life. Write what He shows you for each scripture on the back of each index card.

Vocalize It

Finally, vocalize the scripture and your summary by reading them out loud. Don't be content to think it in your head. There is a place for silent contemplation and reading, but this is not that time. Read the scripture out loud, and then read your summary out loud.

> *We don't fight thoughts effectively with other thoughts, we fight thoughts with words.*

We don't fight thoughts effectively with other thoughts; we fight thoughts with words. If you don't believe this, start counting to twenty in your head, but randomly say your name out loud before you get to twenty. You will find that the second you engage your mouth and speak your name out, the counting in your head stops. The same principle works when renewing your mind with the truth of God's Word. You need to interrupt the trail of thought and re-direct it by using the power of your own voice. It may feel uncomfortable at first, but over time, it will powerfully align your heart and your mind with what God is telling you in and through His Word.

In Matthew 4:10, Jesus got aggressive with the enemy, saying, "Away from me, Satan! For it is written . . ." It's okay to yell sometimes. Aggressively fight the schemes of the enemy. When he "roars" (1 Pet. 5:8), roar back!

Go ahead—read your scripture cards out loud!

Here's a walk-through example of each of the above steps:

You may be struggling with a lie from the enemy that says, "You are not enough" (not successful enough, not handsome or pretty enough, not a good enough spouse or parent, etc.).

Truth of Scripture: "The Lord your God has chosen you out of all the peoples on the face of the earth to be his people, his treasured possession" (Deut. 7:6).

Summarize it: The Israelites were God's chosen people and His treasured possession. Likewise, because of what Christ has done and because I am a part of God's family, I am fully loved, chosen, treasured, and accepted by God. Regardless of how much I feel like I don't measure up or how much I do (or fail to do), I will remain fully loved, chosen, treasured, and accepted by God.

Key 2: Renewing Your Mind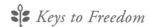

Personalize It: God, thank You for the inheritance and the identity that is mine as Your son/daughter. Thank You that no matter how weak I might be or how often I feel that I don't measure up, my identity is that I am Your beloved. Because of what Jesus has done (and not because of what I have done), I know that I am chosen, treasured, and accepted by You. I have all that I need in You, so I choose to surrender to You and Your ability to complete me and sustain me so that I lack nothing. In You, I am enough, and I have enough. Thank You, Father.

Vocalize: (Say it all out loud!)

Take the truths from God's Word that you are discovering and vocalize them on a daily basis. Every morning during daily Bible reading at the Mercy homes, the residents and staff declare scriptures out loud. (You can find some of these in Appendix C at the back of this study.) Just as God spoke the creation of the world into existence, when you speak His Word out loud, it has power beyond anything you can see. Speaking Scripture out loud plants it inside of you and brings life, because God is literally "watching over [His] word to perform it" (Jeremiah 1:12). As Proverbs 18:21 says, "Death and life are in the power of the tongue, and those who love it will eat its fruit" (ESV).

Renewing your mind to God's Truth is a lifelong process. On our first day of this week's study, we compared our thoughts to hiking trails and discussed how we can actually change the trails of our thought lives. However, just as hiking trails don't disappear overnight but instead disappear over the course of time, it may take some time for us to see our old thought patterns change. But if you take these steps consistently, in one year you will hardly recognize yourself. That transformation will continue, and you will wonder how you came so far so fast. That is the power of agreeing with God — it brings life, peace, and countless blessings.

Instead of the lies of the enemy, how do you think it will feel to live each day with the mind and thoughts of Christ?

Ask the Lord, "Father, what is something that you are most excited about for me as I begin the process of renewing my mind?" Write what He reveals to you below.

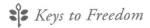 *Keys to Freedom*

Key 2: Renewing Your Mind

JOURNAL

What did God speak or show to you throughout the week?

Don't forget to share what God is doing in your life or any valuable insights you have received.
And be sure to use the #KeystoFreedom hashtag!

Key 3

Healing Life's Hurts

Jason's story

As a child, I had a learning disability that was made all the more challenging by the fact that I had four siblings who were all honor students. Meanwhile, my father was physically, verbally, and emotionally abusive, which made things even more difficult. He often told me that I was not smart enough to go to college.

After graduating from high school, I chose to take a year off of school and work. As that year was coming to a close, I felt led to go to college and major in English, minoring in writing. I remember one night sitting in my bedroom and telling my dad about my plans. His response to me was, "Do you think you would actually be good at that?" That question and the doubt in his voice stung me to my core.

What I couldn't know then was that the pain of my father's words that night would affect me more than I realized. The enemy used that moment to reinforce all of the lies that I had struggled with since childhood. I felt inadequate. I would never measure up. I felt especially "stupid." Those were lies that I continued to struggle with into adulthood. It was a significant area of insecurity for me, and it had been magnified by the memory of what my father had said to me that night in my bedroom.

As the years went on, I began seeing how this insecurity had been affecting my life and molding much of the way I felt and thought on a daily basis. I began seeking healing and freedom through Christian counseling, and a couple of years ago, I attended a conference where they encouraged us to process a painful memory with the Lord, asking the Holy Spirit to show us His perspective on what happened. As we prayed, I saw myself sitting in my bedroom, telling my father my plans for college. I heard him ask again if I actually thought I would be good at that. And then I saw Jesus sitting on my bed holding out a pen and paper to me. He showed me where He was in that moment of pain. He was encouraging me and showing me that He believed in me.

I had experienced a lot of growth in this specific area of struggle through my walk with Christ and through the counseling I'd sought, but this was the final step to true healing. There was such an amazing release of hurt in that moment. Freedom and comfort rushed in and took its place. I was able to reject the lies that I was stupid and inadequate and leave them in the past.

The words that my father spoke to me that night were so painful, but what actually caused me the most long-term harm was the destructive lies that I believed as a result of that pain. I will always be grateful to God for inviting me into a conversation about where He was and what He said about me that night. Now when I encounter moments where I would have typically felt dumb or inadequate, I choose to believe what my Heavenly Father says about me instead of what my earthly father said about me. Those lies just do not carry the weight that they used to carry. God has removed those insecurities, and the memory of what happened that night no longer controls me. I'm not perfect, but I am healed. And it's from a place of healing that I have seen transformation take place in my life.

 *Keys to Freedom* — Key 3: Healing Life's Hurts

Day 1: *When Life Hurts*

Every one of us experiences hurt. When those hurts remain unhealed, they can cause us to shrink back from life, to operate out of fear, and to build our lives around avoiding more hurt. We take fewer healthy risks in relationships, jobs, and ministry. Some people have been so hurt in the past that they sabotage relationships because they don't think they deserve them. Others who have been hurt by abandonment or loss will cling to friends and loved ones too tightly or accuse those around them of not being faithful enough. Any person who has an unhealed hurt will find their decision-making negatively impacted. It's like the tree that we described in the first chapter; every negative root of fear or rejection or abandonment feeds our beliefs, which in turn sustains the branches of our behaviors.

Why do you think suffering deep hurts can have such a strong effect on our decisions?

The enemy's plan is to use your hurts to hold you back. He wants to put boundaries on your life based on your fear of being hurt again. Total freedom means no longer allowing hurts to direct our lives, tarnish our relationships, and shape our personalities. Many people don't want to acknowledge their hurts because of the painful emotions attached to them. Instead of running to God, they run away from Him to hide their shame, much like Adam and Eve did in the Garden of Eden (Genesis 3:7). But you can't run from your hurts because they always catch up. The only safe place to run is into the arms of a loving God.

> *You can't run from your hurts because they always catch up. The only safe place to run is into the arms of a loving God.*

The idea of facing the feelings you carry from the hurts of the past may feel intimidating and overwhelming. Some people conclude that because they have been so hurt, no emotions can be trusted. They won't even allow themselves to feel happiness or joy because it makes them feel out of control. The idea of going back to past hurts means unlocking the box with all the emotions in it – a seemingly dangerous and scary idea.

How does the thought of going back to face past hurts cause you to feel? Why?

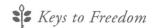

While the idea of facing those hurts from the past may stir up a variety of emotions, the truth is that pouring out our emotions to God is where inner healing begins. We encourage you to consider doing this with a Christian counselor, pastor, or mentor if you feel it's appropriate for your situation (i.e. when the memories of the past are particularly traumatic or trigger you). However, for most people, pouring out our hearts to God and allowing Him to speak into the hurtful and painful experiences of our past is a very simple and effective exercise.

Read Psalm 142:1-2. How is God the ultimate Counselor and "prayer partner" with whom to process your hurts?

Being open and honest with the Lord is vital in helping us move forward. God is not afraid or offended by our anger, our disappointment, or our confusion, even if it is directed at Him. He can handle our emotions. We have a choice in whether or not we will express our hurt openly and honestly. The good news is that Jesus has a response to our pain, anger, and disappointment. He has something to say about the situations we have faced and the damage we have sustained. His heart desire is to bring healing and to show us His perspective. He wants to let us know that He was never the source of our pain, but He will be the source for our healing if we allow Him to be.

While we don't base our choices on emotions or allow them to lead out, God does give us emotions to enjoy. Some emotions are meant to signal that something is going on inside of us that needs to be addressed. Those signals may be in the form of paralyzing fear, deep hurt, or uncontrollable anger. Even God himself has emotions. Jesus experienced the whole range of human emotions during His earthly life.

Read each of the passages below and list the emotion(s) Jesus experienced in each one.

Matthew 14:14 _____

Mark 3:5 _____

Luke 10:21 _____

 *Keys to Freedom* Key 3: Healing Life's Hurts

John 11:35 _____

Mark 10:21 _____

The Bible promises, "We do not have a high priest who is unable to empathize with our weaknesses, but we have one who has been tempted in every way, just as we are—yet he did not sin. Let us then approach God's throne of grace with confidence, so that we may receive mercy and find grace to help us in our time of need" (Heb. 4:15–16). Jesus sympathizes with every weakness we have. He experienced every hurt, pain, and disappointment that we experience – either while He was walking the earth or on the cross. Jesus desires to meet us and heal us from a place of compassion and care because He understands.

Take a couple of moments to ask the Lord what He has to share with you about the emotions connected to any of the unhealed hurts in your life. What is His promise to you regarding your healing process?

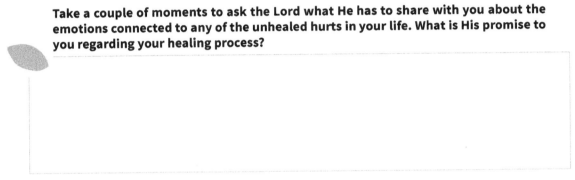

When we keep all of our emotions inside, we can't grow in intimacy with Him. He is the only one who can bear our hurts and help us to heal. He won't force it. Jesus is a gentleman and very gentle with us. He simply waits for us to invite Him to come and heal our hearts.

Day 2: *Emotions Are Not the Enemy*

We closed yesterday's time together by talking about the importance of pouring our emotions out to God. We discussed how He is the only one who can fully bear our hurts and help us heal.

What does Psalm 91:4 say that God will do for us?

Key 3: Healing Life's Hurts 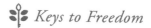 Keys to Freedom

Vulnerability may seem risky, but with God there is safety. You can relax knowing that God is trustworthy. He will never hurt you. He wants to heal the wounds that have kept you bound. Isaiah 53:5 says, "But He was wounded for our transgressions; He was bruised for our iniquities; the chastisement for our peace was upon Him, and by His stripes we are healed" (NKJV). That healing includes the hurts from our past.

What are God's promises to us in Isaiah 61:1-3? Write them in your own words in the space below.

Do you honestly believe that God can take the hurts of your past and give you beauty, gladness, and praise in their place? Do you feel like you can trust Him with your hurts? Why or why not? Explain.

You are allowed to cry. There can be great release in tears. It is normal to feel hurt, angry, or cheated. Jesus Himself wept publicly, which tells us it can be emotionally healthy to do so. Your emotions help you to acknowledge the truth of the hurt you experienced and allow Jesus to heal your heart.

Our emotions act as signposts along the road of life. They indicate where we find ourselves in relation to what is happening. For example, if you lose a loved one, the signpost may say "sadness" or "anger." It's healthy to experience the vast array of emotions. It is normal to feel hurt, angry, or cheated. When Lazarus died in John 11, Jesus wept. He allowed the signpost called "sadness" to be seen and heard, even though He knew that He would soon resurrect Lazarus and move past that signpost and bring healing. Jesus valued the emotion enough to allow it a moment to be expressed and modeled to us. The damage comes when we hold onto emotions or don't allow them to be expressed. We think shutting them down or ignoring them makes them go away, but instead we stay parked at the signpost and that emotion becomes a destination. Sadness is not a good place to live, nor is anger or disappointment. Expressing your emotions helps you to acknowledge the truth of what you experienced, or are experiencing, and then you can invite Jesus in to heal you.

What does Jesus tell us to do in Matthew 11:28?

By holding on to your pain, you are denying Him the opportunity to comfort you and take that heavy burden from you. If you don't take the step to come to Him, He can't give you the rest and healing that He has for you.

> *Shakespeare famously wrote that the "truth will out." That's true of hurts too. They will express themselves one way or another.*

Some people bury their hurts deep in a futile attempt to keep those wounds from affecting their present-day life. But hurts just can't be forgotten. Shakespeare famously wrote that the "truth will out." That's true of hurts, too. They will express themselves one way or another.

How have the hurts you've experienced expressed themselves? For instance, are you easily frustrated or angered around certain people or in certain situations? Are there subjects you just won't think about or places you won't go because the memory is too painful? List anything that comes to mind in the space below.

There are many healthy ways to express our emotions and everyone has their own preferences. For you, it might be journaling, taking a walk, poetry, singing, art, or writing a letter to the person that hurt you and tearing it up. Part of this process for you may be discovering ways that help you personally.

Key 3: Healing Life's Hurts  Keys to Freedom

Invite the Lord into the details that you shared on the last question. Ask Him to show you what He wants you to know and to give you His perspective. Write what He shows you below.

Day 3: *Connecting with Our Hurts*

Healing from hurts means going back to where things started. We are going to spend today and tomorrow discussing a process that can be helpful in praying through the hurts of your past. As you pray through hurts, allow God into those parts of your life, giving Him the opportunity to bring healing and restoration. You may also want to consider doing this exercise with a Christian counselor, pastor, or mentor if you feel it is appropriate for your situation.

You will want to have some time and space set aside over these next couple of days that you know won't be interrupted. Have paper and a pen on hand to write down what the Lord reveals to you. Sometimes playing soft worship music is helpful as well.

Open each day with prayer, asking God to be with you during your time of processing. Remember that the Holy Spirit should be leading this time. Be sure that you are mindful to allow Him to bring up the hurt that He desires to address. This will safeguard you from trying to pray through hurts that you may not be ready or equipped to address yet. Process the following statements with the Lord in prayer.

Lord, what is one hurt from my past that You desire to heal? Write what He shows you below. This memory may be something you think of often or that you forgot you had even experienced.

Lord, some of the things I remember about that memory are...

I remember that I felt...

What do You want me to know about this memory, Father?

We will continue to pray through this memory tomorrow. However, before you end your study time for today, take some time to sit in the Lord's presence and allow Him to minister to your heart as you prepare to process this hurt with Him tomorrow.

Key 3: Healing Life's Hurts  Keys to Freedom

Day 4: *Facing Our Hurts*

Yesterday you started the process of Healing Life's Hurts by identifying a hurt in prayer and allowing the Lord to bring some of the specific feelings and details of that memory to mind. Allowing the Lord to lead this time of prayer is imperative and will protect and cover your heart as you seek Him for healing.

You may want to go back and review the statements that you processed yesterday. Then continue praying through the memory by asking God the following questions.

Father, thank You for bringing this specific memory to my mind yesterday for healing. I submit that experience to You and ask You to continue the work that You started in my heart.

Lord, how did this memory affect me?

Holy Spirit, will you show me if there was a lie (or lies) that I believed about You or about myself as a result of this hurt?

What is Your truth, Father?

Lord, I choose to break agreement with the lie that _____ , and I choose to believe the truth of _____ .

Father, how do You see me? What do You want me to know about myself?

Holy Spirit, is there anything else You would like me to know or see about this memory? Anything else You want me to break in prayer or release to You?

Finally, release the memory to God, and ask Him to heal you to the root of the hurt. Now that you have a tool to pray through life's hurts, you have the ability to repeat this process for any memory or hurt that the Lord brings to mind in the future.

Day 5: *Moving Forward*

One of the counselors at Mercy has a regular habit that is very healthy. When she feels herself getting uptight, irritable, and easily offended, she takes some time to sit down and pray through her hurts. It often starts with a question: "God, I've been feeling uptight and angry about things recently. Why is that?" Sitting quietly, she often hears the still, small voice of the Holy Spirit pointing out things in her life that are bothering her. She writes them down on a piece of paper, says them out loud, and then forgives people

Key 3: Healing Life's Hurts 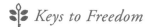 Keys to Freedom

and asks forgiveness of God for her own attitude. She then tears up the paper as a symbol of forgetting those hurts and spends time in worship to let God minister to her. That is a simple way you can address your own hurts – not just the old, deep ones but also the fresh, new ones that happen throughout the day.

Healing past hurts is a critical part of maintaining freedom even in difficult circumstances.

Look up 2 Corinthians 5:17, and write it in your own words below. What does it tell us happens when we are in Christ?

As children of God, we have a choice in allowing the newness of who we are in Christ to empower us to address and move on from the old hurts of the past.

What will life look like when you are healed of the hurts you still feel? For instance, what will you do differently? What will your attitude about the future be like? Will you attempt more and do more? Will you treat people better? List anything that comes to mind.

> *As children of God, we have a choice in allowing the newness of who we are in Christ to empower us to on from the old hurts of the past.*

Now, ask the Lord to give you a word or a picture that represents what your life will look like on the other side of healing. What did He show you? Write it out below.

Study Guide | 67

 *Keys to Freedom* Key 3: Healing Life's Hurts

You may have been living in emotional survival mode for years, feeling that you had to take care of yourself and deal with your own pain without trusting anyone along the way. God not only listens to your heart and heals your wounds, but He will teach you how to continue to address the hurts that are inevitable this side of Heaven. He is trustworthy. He will relieve you of your burdens as you lay them down at the feet of Jesus. Hold tightly to the Bible's promises.

Write Psalm 18:2 in the space below.

Don't spend one more day letting your past hurts lead the way. Face those hurts, and recognize God's faithfulness in your past and present, moving ahead with confidence.

JOURNAL

What did God speak or show to you throughout the week?

Don't forget to share what God is doing in your life or any valuable insights you have received. And be sure to use the #KeystoFreedom hashtag!

Key 4
Choosing to Forgive

Heather's Story

I remember the day the journey of true forgiveness started. Don't get me wrong, I wanted to start many times before, but I just couldn't get to the place of feeling "ready" enough. It was one of my biggest frustrations - the tension between wanting to forgive in the hope of greater freedom and not feeling ready enough to let go and risk being hurt or disappointed again. The anger and pain over what had happened to me had become a comfort; it reminded me that what happened was real and drove me to be strong, to overcome, and to protect myself from harm.

Years later, when I could no longer be satisfied with the stalemate I had found myself in, I applied for the Mercy program. It was within the walls of this beautiful place that I finally came face to face with the truth about forgiveness. As I sat in a group counseling session, I heard the group leader speak these words: "Forgiveness is not a feeling, it's a choice."

"What!?" the word had escaped my lips before I even realized it, and the group leader looked me in the eyes and repeated her statement. It was a simple yet profound truth; so simple I needed to hear it twice! Yet while it was simple, it was not easy. I realized in that moment that I held the key to my own freedom, and in order to unlock my pain, I would need to face it. The truth was that I might never come to the point of feeling ready. Forgiveness was a simple, yet costly choice, and I had to trust that the feelings would follow that choice.

I was beginning to understand that if I was going to choose to forgive, I needed to acknowledge what I was forgiving. My heart was beating in my chest; as memories arose, my fists were clenched, but my mind was made up. I spoke each word out loud as testimony to God and to myself of the decision I was making, and I released forgiveness to my abuser through gritted teeth. I made the decision that I would choose to continue to forgive my abuser, and all those who had hurt me, until my life overflowed with forgiveness. The next day, I returned to that same spot, and I released forgiveness again and the next day and the next, and the next. After some time, I noticed a difference in my prayers and in my countenance. Where previously I had forced each word from my mouth, now my words flowed easily, and I found myself releasing not only forgiveness to my abuser, but compassion and a prayer for his salvation! This was not an attempt to feel healed; this was an overflow of healing ushered in through my choice to forgive.

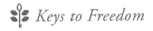 Keys to Freedom   Key 4: Choosing to Forgive

Day 1: *The Power of Forgiveness*

Have you ever considered the oyster? Oysters are the living organisms responsible for producing pearls. Oysters live in harsh terrain – in the ocean or in rivers where all sorts of dangers lurk. Grains of sand, parasites, or sharp pieces of shell can find their way past the oyster's hard outer shell and into the fleshy, soft tissue of the living organism. When this happens, the oyster has a brilliant way of responding to the intrusion: it produces something called nacre (nā'kər).

Nacre is sometimes known as "mother of pearl" in reference to the fact that the very substance of a pearl is made up of layer upon layer of nacre. So oysters can turn an obstruction, an irritant, and a violation into a precious jewel by secreting this substance and covering the irritant, rounding off its sharp edges, until it can no longer cause damage.

Sadly, only about 50% of oysters that have an irritant or obstruction lodged inside of them produce a pearl. When an oyster fails to produce nacre, it risks everything. The obstruction, whether it's a grain of sand or a small piece of broken shell, will often have sharp edges, so it will begin to cut away and erode the soft tissue — the living part of the oyster. Or if it's a parasite that enters, it will gradually gnaw away at the inside of the oyster until there is nothing left. It will slowly erode and eventually become nothing but an empty shell.

Much like the oyster, God has created us with the spiritual equivalent of nacre. We have an inner ability to respond to pain, hurt, offense, trauma, and abuse that will cause these violations to halt their destructive path on the inside of us; it's called forgiveness. The oyster's strategy of defending itself against something that has lodged within its core is probably one of the clearest metaphors regarding forgiveness.

> *We may not be able to choose what happens to us, but we can choose how we will respond.*

We all live in an environment where the same grains of sand that can kill an oyster can make their way inside of us and begin to cause damage. For us, those grains of sand can be offense, neglect, betrayal, abuse, disappointment, sin, lies, grief, gossip…the list goes on. The fact is that life can be harsh, and it's inevitable that we will suffer some degree of hurt and pain along the way. But the level of damage we sustain is not dependent on the severity of the offense; it's dependent on our response to it. We may not be able to choose what happens to us, but we can choose how we will respond.

An oyster can be killed by something as small as one piece of sand or as large as a parasite. Either way, the end result is death on the inside. The life-saving response is nacre; and one of the most vital nacre responses we can have is forgiveness. To choose not to forgive is to choose to allow the process of bitterness and resentment to slowly kill you from the inside out. If you choose to forgive, you choose life, freedom, and hope.

Look up the following scriptures. What do they tell us?

Matthew 5:44–45

Luke 6:37

Romans 12:17

Colossians 3:13

Forgiveness is part of God's heart towards us. It's in His nature to forgive. His desire, in fact, His commandment, is that we also forgive – not because He wants to make our lives difficult, but because He knows that forgiveness is a significant key to our walking in wholeness and freedom. If the idea of forgiving those who have hurt you is overwhelming right now, don't be discouraged! We are going to spend this week unpacking some of the myths of forgiveness and allowing the Lord to speak and minister to our hearts in regards to this powerful, but sometimes challenging, key to freedom.

Day 2: *Forgiving God*

One of the basic deceptions, and most effective traps, of the enemy is to cause people to confuse his work with God's will. The enemy deceives people into thinking God is the author of evil things that happen. It is one of the enemy's deadliest tools against the children of God because if you think God is the source of your pain, He cannot be the resource for your healing.

When people believe that God hurt them, it creates a huge wedge in their relationship with Him. Can you imagine loving, trusting, and worshipping a God who planned and caused your deepest pain? When people who have been hurt hear that God has a plan for their lives, they often say, "If God's plan looks like what I've experienced, I don't want anything to do with Him."

Let's be really clear: There are two plans for your life. God has a plan for you, and the enemy has a plan for you. And they couldn't be more opposed to one another.

According to John 10:10, what is God's plan for you? What is the enemy's plan?

One of the biggest hang-ups people often have, as they break free from past hurts and learn to walk in freedom, is their offense toward God. Deep down, many people believe God has treated them or someone they love in a neglectful or unfair way, so they choose to ignore Him. They are, in effect, punishing God for what they believe He did "wrong" by giving Him the silent treatment and deliberately remaining distant and angry. If your perception of Him is that He has let you down or disappointed you, don't be afraid to tell Him that.

It's important that we understand that God is more than able to handle every bit of your darkest emotions towards Him. We know that God is good and only does good. However, you may be living with the perception that He has wronged you. So your choice to let out your emotions to Him and, in essence, "forgive" Him will help position you to hear what He has to say about those experiences and hurts.

Do you have a grudge against God? Are you holding Him responsible for some injustice you or someone you love suffered? Explain.

Key 4: Choosing to Forgive 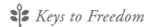 Keys to Freedom

There's a simple exercise you can do to examine how you see God. The purpose is to shed light on your relationship and the posture of your heart towards Him. Some people may picture God sitting on a throne, and they see themselves close to Him. Others see themselves very far away from Him. Some see Him as a good father and some as a threatening authority figure.

Ask the Lord to show you a picture that represents the way you see Him. Once you have received this picture from Him, write down what you saw below.

In the picture, what was your physical posture towards Him? Were you close to Him or far away?

What was your emotional posture toward Him? What feelings came up when He showed you this picture?

Your response to these questions will tell you a lot about your relationship with God. When you open up the lines of communication with Him and tell Him how you really feel, you will find that He will speak directly to your heart and situation in such a way that brings healing and restoration.

Never in the Bible is anything good attributed to Satan, and the Bible tells us with absolute certainty that God is perfect in love. He has never done a wrong thing. He has only done good to you since the day you were conceived. That means it was never in God's will that you be hurt or rejected or scarred by another person. His love for you is so great that He sent Jesus to pay the penalty for your sins and take the pain away from you. His heart was broken, so yours could be healed. Now He wants to give back to you everything the enemy has stolen.

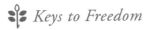 *Keys to Freedom*   Key 4: Choosing to Forgive

People so often get caught up in the why: "Why did this happen to me? Why did God allow it?" The answer is simple: Someone did evil to you, you chose evil for yourself, or evil simply happened because we live in a fallen world. However, God did not abandon us to this evil. He has equipped us to respond with good. Through Jesus Christ and the power of forgiveness, we are able to completely disempower the enemy's effect of evil in our lives. We just have to make the choice to do it!

> *Through Jesus Christ and the power of forgiveness, we are able to completely disempower the enemy's effect of evil in our lives.*

Let's take a moment to officially shut this door of deception. Say this out loud:

God is never bad.
The enemy is never good.

Again, John 10:10 states very clearly: "The enemy comes only to steal, kill and destroy; I have come that you may have life, and have it to the full!" God is not the author of your pain. He is the author of your deliverance and joy. The enemy is the enemy, not God. We don't base this truth on our own opinions but on the sure Word of God.

Day 3: *The Strength to Forgive Ourselves*

Before we can even talk about how to forgive others, we must understand the depth to which God has forgiven us! The Bible tells us that God keeps no record of your wrongs. Hebrews 8:12 says, "For I will forgive their wickedness and will remember their sins no more." All He asks is that you recognize your sin, confess to Him, and commit to turn from that sin. It's so difficult for our minds to comprehend that He keeps no record of sins, but it's true!

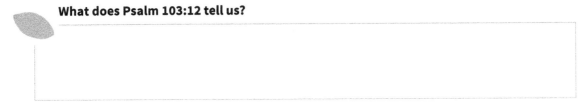

What does Psalm 103:12 tell us?

The most amazing thing happened the day Jesus died on the cross: God's wrath and judgment toward all of the sins you have ever committed and all of the sins you will ever commit were placed on Jesus. When we give our lives to Him, we have to start believing we are who God says we are. He tells us that in Christ, we are forgiven, free, and pure!

Key 4: Choosing to Forgive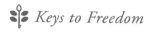

What thoughts or emotions come up for you when you think about the fact that God has totally forgiven your sins and rebellion against Him? Is it difficult for you to truly believe? If so, why?

Our ability to fully forgive is fueled and strengthened by our knowledge of the depth to which we have been forgiven ourselves. Some of us may be able to accept and believe the fact that God has forgiven us, but we have a hard time forgiving ourselves. We may feel as if we are more in control and even experience a sense of safety by remaining angry with ourselves, but that control is not real and erodes quickly. We must learn to not only receive grace from God but also extend that grace to ourselves.

> *Our ability to fully forgive is fueled and strengthened by our knowledge of the depth to which we have been forgiven ourselves.*

Why do you think the enemy wants to keep us from forgiving ourselves?

We may feel exposed and vulnerable in the process of forgiving ourselves and lying our past before God, but this is the time to rely even more on the Lord's comfort and strength. God sent His only Son to this world to die so that we could be free from sin. When we do not forgive ourselves, we are essentially saying that Jesus' death on the cross is not enough for us. Forgiving yourself is no easy task, but the freedom that follows is immeasurable. Trust Him with your hurts and those things you feel so ashamed about. The enemy cannot make unclean what God has made clean, so let go of the shame and receive what God has done!

Ask the Lord, "Jesus, is there an area where I have not fully forgiven myself? If so, what is it?" Write what He shows you below.

Study Guide

 Keys to Freedom

Then, make the decision to fully let it go by praying this prayer:

Father, I ask you to forgive me and cleanse me for _____ . Also, I choose to fully forgive myself and surrender this area of my life to you. I receive your forgiveness and cleansing. Thank you for forgiving me and cleansing me from all unrighteousness, in Jesus' Name. Amen.

Day 4: *Obstacles to Forgiveness*

God's forgiveness towards us is intertwined with our forgiveness of others. This is why without forgiveness, true freedom is impossible to attain. In order for us to receive God's forgiveness, we must forgive others. It's the only way to live free of the hurt of the past and the bitterness and resentment that comes in when we do not forgive.

Before we discuss forgiving others, let's look at some of the obstacles, or myths, that people face in relation to forgiveness and address each one:

"If I forgive, I am saying that what happened was okay."

Sometimes, we resist forgiveness because it can feel as if we are saying that what happened to us was okay. But forgiveness does not place a stamp of approval on the offense, and in truth, forgiveness is not about those who have hurt you; it's about you. As we acknowledge unforgiveness and look at the full impact of our hurt, we can work through the painful memories and reach a place of forgiveness.

Forgiveness is the mechanism whereby we say, "What you did is not okay, but the judgement of your behavior belongs to God, not to me." In making this choice, we hand over the desire for revenge to the Lord, and we trust Him to be the God of Justice in our situation.

It's also important to note that while forgiveness is not earned, trust is. We are not expected to blindly trust someone who has hurt us. That is both naïve and irresponsible! You wouldn't hand a key to your house over to a thief. As such, forgiving a wrong does not mean extending the person an invitation to hurt you again.

Forgiveness isn't the same as reconciliation. Yes, forgiveness may be the start of reconciliation, but there

Key 4: Choosing to Forgive 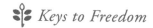 Keys to Freedom

are times when reconciliation is not possible. It's not necessary to seek reconciliation when the other person is unrepentant, unchanging, and/or unsafe for you. You can still release forgiveness towards those who have hurt you while also putting up healthy boundaries in your life.

"I will never be able to forget what happened, so I can't forgive it."

God asks us to forgive, not forget. Even if we could, it wouldn't be wise to erase from our memory all the wrongs done to us and by us. If we did, we would never learn from our experiences and would be caught in a perpetual cycle of reliving the same situations, fears, disappointments, and abuse. However, what can be healed — and is, in fact, one of the things that forgiveness releases — is the damaging effect of the raw emotions associated with the events. As we commit to releasing the nacre of forgiveness, the sharp edges of that violation or offense are covered to the point where they can cause no more damage, and the pain caused by those events can be healed.

Write Genesis 50:20 in the space below.

When we walk in obedience, God has a way of bringing good out of the most difficult and hurtful situations. Forgiveness is often a part of that obedience. It takes the sting out of the painful memory and turns into good what the enemy meant for evil.

"I don't feel like forgiving."

At the beginning of this week, Heather shared that her process of forgiveness started with a choice, not a feeling. Forgiveness rarely comes from feelings. In fact, during the process of forgiveness, our feelings will often work against us. If we wait until we feel like forgiving, it may never happen. Forgiveness is a choice that comes from a decision to walk in obedience to the Word of God.

> *If we wait until we feel like forgiving it may never happen. Forgiveness is a choice that comes from a decision to walk in obedience to the Word of God.*

One of the best ways to make forgiving easier is to remind ourselves that people are not our enemy. Our enemy is the enemy. People often act in ignorance or plain blind selfishness. The people who hurt you were motivated and urged on by the enemy, sometimes against their better judgment and sometimes in blindness to the consequences.

However, as you continually make the choice to forgive, the Lord will honor your obedience, and your feelings will start to change over time. Considering the level at which you may have been hurt, forgiveness may sound crazy to you right now, but we have seen time and time again that making the daily choice to forgive, eventually leads to a heart shift and the feelings follow the choice. Your heart is no longer stuck in the hurt and is actually healed by your choice to forgive. The Lord doesn't command us to forgive just to make our lives difficult. He knows that walking the hard road of forgiveness is the only way for our hearts to arrive at a place of healing and wholeness.

"I can't forgive until the person who hurt me apologizes."

When the individual that hurt us shows no remorse and seems to have moved on with their life, it can be difficult to let an offense or hurt go. Whether the other person has asked for your forgiveness or not, we must remember that forgiving someone is an act of obedience. But as you have learned by now, forgiveness is not an emotional decision and may not even "feel" fair. If we wait for an apology to forgive, we may wait forever, and in the meantime, our lives are the ones being affected by unforgiveness, not the people who have hurt us. Whether or not we have received an apology, the Lord is faithful to empower us to do what He has asked of us.

Ask, "Holy Spirit, have I been hindered in the area of forgiveness by any of the myths that were discussed today? If so, how? What would You like me to do about that?" Write out what He reveals to you below.

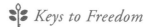

Day 5: *Forgiving Those Who Hurt You*

By now, you have hopefully recognized that forgiveness is serious stuff. Forgiveness is literally the power to overcome what the enemy meant for harm. He wants the ripple effect of hurt and abuse to go on for generations. You may have heard the saying, "Hurt people hurt people." That is the enemy's design. But God has put it within our grasp to stop the enemy's plan by forgiving. Just as we are saved by faith and not feelings, so also are we empowered to forgive by faith and not feelings. We can forgive without even wanting to! In fact, that's exactly how it works – by choice.

Today we will spend some time with God talking about a specific person who hurt us. As you spend this time in prayer, we encourage you to remember that you can be honest with God. He can carry the weight of it.

Many people wonder what they are supposed to do when they want to forgive someone but are still angry. Yelling can be a form of prayer! God is not afraid of volume. Your words and tone might frighten you, but they will not frighten Him. He knows those things are inside of you already, and it's a lot better to get them out than to let them continue to fester. If you have a sincere desire to connect with God and are not just indulging your bitterness and making the problem worse, then airing your emotions to Him can move you toward freedom and a stronger relationship with Him.

Ask the Lord to show you someone who has hurt you and the specific offense. Then write down any thoughts and feelings you might have about that person and the offense.

Now take a moment to say a prayer of forgiveness for this person. You may choose to use the prayer on the following page, but the choice and the act of forgiveness is more important than the words you use to do it.

Prayer:

Father, I come before You now, and I ask that You would help me to forgive. Help me to be free from what has happened to me, as well as the pain and thoughts that come with this hurt. Lord, I pray that You would make a way where there seems to be no way. I choose to forgive _____ for _____ . (List the name of the person you need to forgive and what you are forgiving them for). I release forgiveness in the Name of Jesus. I release them from their debt to me and place them in Your hands. I declare that this act of my will and obedience will produce in me a pearl of great value, a heart that is free and wounds that are healed. In the Name of Jesus, I pray, Amen.

When you forgive, you do what Jesus did and gain ultimate freedom. As you do so, your feelings may be pulling you in the opposite direction. You have the opportunity to choose obedience over your emotions. Ultimately, the power to forgive is not of ourselves. It is God working in us as we choose to walk in His truth, often in spite of our feelings.

> *When you forgive, you do what Jesus did and gain ultimate freedom.*

Forgiveness opens the door to restoration and freedom for you and possibly even for the person you have chosen to forgive. The way you handle unfairness can be a powerful example for others to follow. It can literally transform the lives of those around you.

As we move forward in this study, remember that forgiveness is not something you do just to be free from your past; forgiveness is a way of life. People will hurt and upset you, overlook you, and let you down. You will make mistakes and let others down too, but forgiveness is the nacre that flows through your life to keep each of those "painful" moments from being the start of a deeper root. So while forgiving the "big" things is important, it's also the day-to-day forgiveness that protects our hearts.

Let's close this week by reviewing the powerful words of Romans 12:17-21. Read this passage, and then write out verse 21 in the space below.

The only way to overcome evil is with good. The only way to overcome hatred and hurt is with love. Ultimately, it is only after we recognize that we have been forgiven much that we will have what we need to love much (Luke 7:47). And living in love is what living in freedom is all about.

Key 4: Choosing to Forgive  Keys to Freedom

JOURNAL

What did God speak or show to you throughout the week?

Don't forget to share what God is doing in your life or any valuable insights you have received. And be sure to use the #KeystoFreedom hashtag!

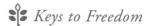

Key 5
Breaking Generational Patterns

Richard's Story

At 21, I married a wonderful woman with whom I could build a life and family. We were young, and as marriage tends to do, it turned the spotlight on our character flaws and issues. I found myself tripping over the same issues again and again in my life. Life was a mini rollercoaster of emotion, and I did not seem to be in charge of the pace. It became obvious that I was angry pretty much all of the time. I did not like the control that this emotion had over my actions and me, but I didn't know what to do with it.

As things got worse, I was determined to find help because I have always been a firm believer that "what you don't deal with, your kids will have to deal with." My wife had suggested that I would benefit from some ministry and some time away to pray through situations that had left me wounded. I didn't want to go. I didn't feel like I was that messed up. But after I thrashed it out with God, I booked myself a weeklong ministry retreat two hundred miles from home. I did not want my children to carry the same weight and burdens that I did, so the answer was simple: swallow my pride and start the journey to become what God had asked me to be, a great husband and great father.

During my time at the retreat, the leaders asked questions about my father, his father, and his father before him. They were finding where the wounds in our family were first created, so they could be healed. My grandfather had made some choices in his life that allowed a lot of hurt and trauma into our family. The effects of that trauma were passed on to my father. And that was passed on to me. My father did not intend for this to happen, but a wounded man will wound others. This was a pattern, and I could see clearly how that pattern had been affecting me for years.

God helped me to identify the patterns that were active in my life, and He showed me the truth of His Word, so I could start to live free. I could see so clearly where my issues had come from, and how I had been influenced by what had been modeled to me. Over the course of the next few days, those specific patterns were prayed through and broken. Healing came, and for the first time, I felt I had an opportunity to rewrite history.

On the way home, I remember my wife saying that I looked visibly different and that my face had changed. I felt healed in so many areas. I no longer felt angry or trapped. But it was still a process. Though I had prayed and specifically broken the relevant generational patterns, I now had to learn a new way of approaching life. What I noticed was that where I used to find myself behaving in a certain way, breaking those patterns created room for me to hear the voice of God before I acted in the heat of the moment. Now I was able to make a choice for myself, rather than be subject to a pattern of behavior. Looking back, the prayer I said wasn't complicated and breaking the patterns wasn't difficult. But I never could have guessed how incredibly necessary and powerful it would be for my family and for me.

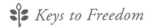 Keys to Freedom Key 5: Breaking Generational Patterns

Day 1: *Your New Bloodline*

Have you ever heard of the saying: "Monkey see, monkey do?" It's a way of describing the natural cycle of a generational pattern - the fact that we are predisposed to becoming what has been modeled to us. This is not just a phenomenon in animals but people as well.

There's a story about a dog that worked in the canine unit of the police force. Her job was to chase down perpetrators and assist the police in arrests. She was the fastest dog in the force, until disaster struck one night. She was chasing a criminal when he ran out onto the road, and as she followed, she was hit by a truck and almost killed. They would have put her down out of kindness, but they discovered at the vet's office that she was carrying a litter of puppies. So they committed to rehabilitating her for the sake of her puppies. She was unable to walk properly due to her injuries – taking two steps with her front paws and dragging her back legs along behind. When her puppies were born, her caregivers were delighted to discover that each one was fully mobile and healthy despite the trauma their mother had suffered. However, within weeks of their birth, the caregivers found a strange thing happening. The puppies, which were born perfectly able to walk, began to copy their mother. Two steps, drag. Two steps, drag. The influence of their mother's injury was so strong that it began to override their own healthy bodies and ability. In the end, the puppies had to be shown by other dogs how to walk so that they would not be limited by an injury that wasn't their own.

This story perfectly illustrates what can happen to us when we are caught in a generational pattern cycle. Let's say, for example, that you were raised in a household where the pressures of life and stress were dealt with by drinking alcohol. The very first time you experience your own stress and pressure in life, you may be tempted to turn to the same (or similar) coping mechanism that was modeled to you. Without realizing it, we typically adopt our parents' and grandparents' approach to life – both the positive and negative traits. We are also influenced by the culture around us, the society in which we live, and the belief system it holds. It's important to add that generational patterns apply to everyone – even if you do not know your biological family or have no biological children of your own.

> *The power to change is in your spiritual bloodline.*

The good news is that Jesus' perfect human life made possible a "second birth." Through His blood, a new bloodline was created that we can enter when we choose to accept the salvation He paid for on the cross.

The power to change is in your spiritual bloodline. In John 3:5-6, Jesus tells a man named Nicodemus, "No one can enter the kingdom of God unless they are born of water and the Spirit. Flesh gives birth to flesh, but the Spirit gives birth to spirit." When we come to Christ, we are literally born again by the Spirit. This is not just a nice metaphor or word picture. It is an actual reality. It takes place in the spirit, meaning we cannot see it, but it is more powerful than our earthly bloodline.

Key 5: Breaking Generational Patterns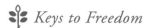

We enter into the family of God through the bloodline of Jesus Christ. His blood is eternal, much stronger than the blood of our earthly families, and has the power to break every negative tendency that comes down to us by genetics or habit. Some of our deepest issues can be rooted in behavioral patterns we didn't create. However, we can control our choices, and as we choose to commit to Christ and be "born again," we literally step into a new bloodline!

Read Galatians 4:4-7. What does it tell you about your position in God's family? Write your thoughts in the space below.

This scripture promises that once we are born again, we become children of God. We enter His bloodline and become co-heirs with Christ. This is the transaction in the spirit that positions us to break the generational patterns that come from our family bloodline and then move forward in freedom.

In Christ, the power of generational patterns is broken. Freedom comes through the power of Christ at work in us now because of our inheritance in Him. We are assured in 1 John 4:4 that, "He who is in you is greater than he who is in the world," (NKJV) and that goes for our family patterns as well.

It's amazing to know that God has given us the power to identify and reject patterns in our family's history and establish new patterns that bring blessing to our future and to the futures of those we influence. We exercise this power when we actively surrender negative generational patterns to God and work to lay a new foundation in Christ.

What thoughts or emotions come to mind as you have learned that you have a new family bloodline in Christ? What does this mean for you and the generations to come after you?

 Keys to Freedom

Key 5: Breaking Generational Patterns

Day 2: *Identifying Negative Patterns*

Whether we like them or not, all of us are affected by the patterns of living and thinking that are passed down to us. These family patterns can be positive or negative, life giving or life destroying. Some family traits give us a great vision for our future. Some threaten to control our lives and even ruin them. Some patterns may be genetic and others behavioral. Our focus today and tomorrow will be on the negative patterns that are passed down in our family line – how to identify and address them.

Negative generational patterns can include things such as the following:

- Arrogance
- Depression
- A hot temper
- Cynicism
- Sense of entitlement
- Poverty mentality
- Unhealthy relationship with food
- Adultery/divorce
- Emotional instability or disconnect from emotions
- Difficulty having close relationships
- Substance abuse
- Independence
- Lack of expression of love or affection
- Different forms of abuse

> *Whether we like them or not, all of us are affected by the patterns of living and thinking that are passed down to us.*

These are just a few examples. There is no exhaustive list as each family establishes its own patterns over generations.

The first step to breaking negative generational patterns is to actually recognize the patterns that were handed down to us through our family bloodline. At Mercy, the residents learn about generational patterns and are often amazed by how these patterns explain their own family history and why they have fallen into the same cycles of sin that previous family members have suffered. The generational patterns in their lives can be a major source of their bondage, but as many of our residents have experienced, once they break and replace destructive generational patterns, many find the old negative patterns turn into

Key 5: Breaking Generational Patterns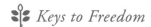

some of their greatest generational blessings.

For example, Krissy grew up in a family that was not emotionally connected or affectionate, so Krissy carried this behavioral pattern without fully recognizing its impact until later in life. As Krissy matured and grew, she started to recognize that she was not "the touchy type" and that she struggled for words to express her care for others. However, she was not faced with the true detriment of this pattern until she got married and had a family. At that point, Krissy's relationship with her husband and children started to be seriously affected by her inability to show or communicate love and care.

If we don't clearly identify the negative patterns in our families, we will never address them and will miss the opportunity to experience victory over them.

With this in mind, ask the Lord to reveal one negative pattern from your family line. Keep in mind that families are made up in many different ways. You may want to consider an extended family member who has had a strong influence in your life. If you have been adopted, you may want to reflect on a pattern in your adoptive family. Write what He reveals to you below.

How has this pattern affected you? Consider the tree diagram, and, perhaps, look back to see if any of the behaviors/belief system/root causes are connected to the generational pattern you've identified.

How has this pattern affected others in your family?

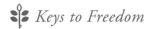

Key 5: Breaking Generational Patterns

Have you noticed the negative pattern appearing in your own life? If so, what will it be like to break free from that pattern?

All families have negative patterns that are passed down. After you identify a negative generational pattern in your family, the next step is to address it in prayer and then in your choices. We will discuss this more tomorrow.

Day 3: *Taking Authority Over Your Family Line*

Once you see specific patterns in your family, you can start exercising the authority and power of choice that flows from your spiritual bloodline as a son or daughter of God. You can stand in the authority He has given you, and choose to break and battle the patterns that He reveals. In doing so, you position your children, both natural and spiritual, to experience a different level of freedom in the areas that you choose to address.

In the Bible, King David fought many wars on every border of his nation. He spent his life destroying Israel's enemies and bringing God's rule and reign into the region. At the end of his life, he was able to hand a kingdom at peace to his son, Solomon. As a result of his father's brave and relentless warrior spirit, King Solomon never had to fight a war. He was handed an inheritance of peace. King Solomon had his own issues to deal with, but he never had to go into battle and defend his territory because his father had fought those battles for him.

> *We are able to fight battles on behalf of those who come after us.*

In the same way, we are able to fight specific battles on behalf of those who come after us. We can be the ones who establish a new pattern of behavior and a new approach to life through Christ Jesus.

Let's look back to Krissy's story from yesterday. Krissy inherited many patterns from the emotionally disconnected environment in which she grew up. Those patterns began to significantly impact her life and relationships. In order to break these patterns of behavior and establish new ones, Krissy would take authority over the patterns by first breaking them in prayer, and then choosing to "step into the battle" to position herself for healing

Key 5: Breaking Generational Patterns 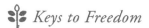 *Keys to Freedom*

and freedom. This included some counseling, learning to label and express her emotions, stepping out and choosing to show more affection, and renewing her mind to the Word. These choices led to the complete breaking of that pattern from Krissy's life, which then created a different environment for her children – one of emotional health and affection. Krissy's children were free from facing that same battle as they grew and matured themselves.

Below, in your own words, write Deuteronomy 30:15–20. How does this apply to our discussion on breaking negative generational patterns?

This scripture tells us that our choices have the ability to lead us to life or death. What choices can you make now to change the negative generational patterns in your family and make choices that lead to life? If you're unsure, ask the Lord to speak to you about this. Write what He shows you below.

As we wrap up today, let's stand in our authority and break the negative generational pattern that the Lord revealed to you yesterday. As you may have noticed by now, any time we break something in prayer (a lie, pattern, etc.), we always replace it with something (truth, a blessing, etc.). Today, we will do the same thing. As you choose to break a negative generational pattern from your family line, you also have the opportunity to ask the Lord to replace it with a generational blessing!

 Key 5: Breaking Generational Patterns

Prayer:

Lord, thank You for revealing to me a negative generational pattern that has existed in my family line. Also, I thank You for the good things that my family has given to me. Right now, I confess this pattern as the sin that it is and ask for Your forgiveness over me and my family. I ask You to break the pattern of _____ and replace it with the generational blessing of _____. Thank You for breaking me free and pouring out Your blessings and love into my life. In Jesus' Name, Amen.

Remember: just like everything else we have discussed so far in this study, freedom is not found in a one-time prayer. Freedom is found as we choose to surrender and overcome. We therefore do not want to close the day without considering our next steps.

Ask the Lord, "Father, now that I have broken this pattern in prayer, what are my next steps? How do I practically "step into the battle" in this area in order to see the victory for myself and my children?" Write what He reveals to you below.

Day 4: *Identifying Positive Patterns*

Now that we have identified and addressed the negative patterns in our family line, we want to take some time to discuss the positive patterns that are also present for each of us. As we mentioned yesterday, any time we break something in prayer (a lie, pattern, etc.), we always replace it with something (truth, a blessing, etc.). When we are in a healing season, much emphasis is placed on the negative areas we need to address in order to overcome. Of course, this is important and needed, but there is power in recognizing the positive and healthy things along the way as well – whether within us or in the context of generational patterns within our family.

Positive generational patterns can include things such as the following:
- Wisdom
- Ability to show affection
- Fidelity
- Generosity

- Unconditional love
- Strong work ethic
- Righteous living
- Serving Others
- Strong and solid commitment to the Lord
- Loyalty
- Self control

Every individual experiences generational patterns in a different way. Some struggle to identify negative patterns within their family, and others may experience the opposite – a struggle to find anything good or healthy within theirs.

For example, Jemma came from a very destructive family line where addiction, abuse, betrayal, and sexual sin were rampant in every generation. Jemma had her own struggles as well, but after meeting and accepting Jesus into her life, she began to experience new levels of freedom from the extensive patterns that were passed down to her from her family. During her healing process, Jemma learned about generational patterns. As you can imagine, she had no difficulty identifying a list of the negative patterns that needed to be addressed. In fact, looking at the list of negative and broken patterns was overwhelming to her. Jemma found herself asking the Lord, "Is there anything *good* from my family line? Anything at all?" At that moment, the Lord reminded Jemma of how as a child, she often saw her grandmother on her knees. The Lord showed Jemma that her grandmother had prayed for her and for many of her family members – which eventually led Jemma to accept Jesus and start on a new path of freedom and wholeness. This revelation was significant for Jemma and allowed her to continue moving forward in her healing process, knowing that while her family line held a lot of difficulty and brokenness, it also held blessing as well.

This story may or may not resonate with you personally, but it's important to point out that the Lord is able to help us find positive patterns that exist in our family lines, even if it is difficult for us. We must intentionally create space to identify the positive. It positions us to walk in balance in our understanding of the generational patterns in our family and gives us the choice to maintain and nourish the positive for our children and ourselves.

> *We must intentionally create space to identify the positive.*

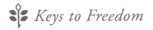

Ask the Lord to reveal to you the positive patterns that exist in your family. For some of you, it may be a list; for others it may be just one. Be honest, and talk with Him through any difficulty you may be experiencing in recognizing the positive patterns in your family.

How can you partner with God to make these generational blessings even more powerful in your life?

Now spend some time thanking Him for those positive patterns. Write anything else that He shows you in the space below.

Day 5: *Freedom for Future Generations*

The freedom available to us as sons and daughters of God is amazing! We are able to address and break destructive patterns in our own lives. Then we are able to position our children for freedom from those same battles. Of all the keys to freedom we discuss in this study, Breaking Generational Patterns is the one that most focuses on the legacy we will leave. This key is always about the next generation, as well as our own personal story.

What do the following verses say about our responsibility to future generations?

Deuteronomy 4:9

Psalm 22:30–31

Have you thought recently about the legacy you desire to leave? Whether or not you have biological children, you will leave a legacy for others from the choices you make and the life that you live. It's significant that we have the choice every day to live in light of the long view and make decisions regarding our legacy. As Abraham Lincoln once said, "In the end, it's not the years in your life that count; it's the life in your years."

What legacy do you want to pass on to the generations after you? How do you hope they describe you and your influence on them?

Keys to Freedom

Key 5: Breaking Generational Patterns

We hope and pray that while you have worked through this study, you have made choices that will build into a beautiful legacy for others. The process is typically never easy, but it always bears good fruit in our lives. Sometimes in that process, though, we need to flip our perspective on our own pain. Our area of struggle can become our area of greatest power and influence in God. Instead of struggling with the difficult details of our history, what if we chose to thank God that we get the opportunity to stand in the gap and turn those patterns around?

Take a couple of moments to thank God for the struggle and the process in your life. Praise Him for His faithfulness and the many ways that He has provided and cared for you. Honor Him for the goodness that is a part of your life and the destiny and legacy that is in His heart for you. Feel free to write down anything that comes to mind in the space below.

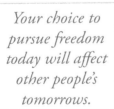

> *Your choice to pursue freedom today will affect other people's tomorrows.*

As you hopefully have learned by now, what you plan and purpose in your heart will affect the generations that follow you. It's not all about here and now; it's also about then and them. Your choice to pursue freedom today will affect other people's tomorrows. Your choice to courageously break old patterns and go after that vision of freedom will go far beyond you.

As we wrap up our discussion on generational patterns and legacy, ask the Lord to show you what you can begin doing today to build the legacy you desire to leave. Record what you believe He shows you below.

Keys to Freedom — Key 5: Breaking Generational Patterns

JOURNAL

What did God speak or show to you throughout the week?

Don't forget to share what God is doing in your life or any valuable insights you have received. And be sure to use the #KeystoFreedom hashtag!

Key 6
Choosing Freedom Over Oppression

Nancy's Story

As a new Christian, I loved life. I felt such freedom in the Lord. I had new friends, new hopes, and a new peace. It came as a total shock when I fell into an eating disorder that turned the next five years of my life into a living hell.

It started one night at my pastor's house. He and his wife graciously invited me over to dinner and served rich Southern foods—fried chicken, biscuits and gravy, and sumptuous desserts. Because the food was so good, I ate a lot that night. Also, I had committed to clean the pastor's house while he and his wife were at a meeting. They left after dinner, and I started cleaning, but my stomach grew increasingly nauseated. Then it hit me: the only way to feel better, so I could finish cleaning, was to make myself throw up. I wasn't even thinking about my weight. I was just determined to keep my commitment. At some point after I had induced vomiting, I heard a voice in my head make a practical suggestion. It said, "You can do that all the time, and you will never, ever have to worry about your weight. You can eat whatever you want—no limits. Just do this every day."

I didn't know it was the voice of the enemy. I was a new Christian and didn't know how to recognize his voice. The suggestion stuck in my mind, and I pondered it and finally agreed with it. In that moment of agreement, I walked directly into a mental and emotional prison. For the next five years, I binged and purged several times a week. It was the worst bondage I have ever experienced. I cried out to God, repented, and fell back into it so many times. I knew that if there were any hope of my being set free, it would be in Christ. How He would release me from this prison, I did not know. I just knew that if I didn't master this thing, it would master me and eventually kill me.

Five years into my struggle, on New Year's Eve, after repenting and failing so many times, I got on my face and said, "God, I'm not moving from this spot until You break this yoke of bondage off of me." I stayed on my face the whole night and begged the Lord, "Tell me what to do to be free from this. I know it's not Your will for me to stay in captivity. Help!" I grabbed onto the promise in Jeremiah 33:3—"Call to Me, and I will answer you, and show you great and mighty things which you do not know" (NKJV)—and held on for dear life.

That night God met me and communicated the truth of what I was going through, and it all seemed so clear. I had been fighting my body, and my body had been fighting back. I was ruining my health, devastating my confidence and peace. Now I knew what the problem was, and I asked God for the solution. He told me very simply, "Eat when you're hungry. Listen to your body. It will tell you what it needs. Eat regular meals, and don't overeat. Your body will burn the food off. Walk three or four times a week for an hour, and don't weigh yourself anymore." His instructions were so basic that it reminded me of Jesus's promise that His yoke is easy and His burden is light. I had turned my life into a maze of rules and restrictions that were running me ragged. His way was so much simpler and better.

I took Him at His word, aimed for total obedience, and gave the outcome to Him. Everything started changing in my body and mind. I felt great peace and freedom. The fear faded away. I didn't have to think all the time about exercise or eating. My health was restored, and my body felt good. God enabled me to escape the oppression and stop being controlled by fear. I learned that when we follow God's path of freedom He takes care of us, both body and soul. We can leave all the results to Him as the good Father He is.

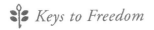 Keys to Freedom   Key 6: Choosing Freedom Over Oppression

Day 1: *Open Doors*

Before we dive into this week's topic, it's really important that we be on the same page about what we are discussing! Various people define oppression in various ways, so we want to be crystal clear about the definition we are using for the sake of our study over the next few days.

We will start by clarifying what we're *not* discussing this week. One definition of the word oppression is "prolonged cruel or unjust treatment." It's the idea of a people group being persecuted or abused. This is not the type of oppression we will be covering in this study.

It's also important to clarify that we are not talking about possession. Oppression and possession are two very different things. To possess something or someone is to take ownership of it, and Satan cannot own anything that belongs to God. When you ask Jesus to be your Savior, you belong to God. You can rest knowing that as you submit your life to Him, the enemy no longer has ultimate power over your life.

However, the enemy can tempt you and apply pressure to your life. In fact, one of the definitions of the word oppression is "pressure," and this is the type of oppression we will be discussing over the course of this week. It's anything that the enemy is able to bring into our lives in the form of habits, addictions, thought patterns, and even unhealthy relationships. Some examples may include: frequent outbursts of anger, low mood/depression, hopelessness, fear, lust, and obsessive thoughts. Severe oppression can render you almost nonfunctional. It feels so heavy and smothering that you can hardly think. People were not created to live under oppression and heaviness, but so many do, and they don't know how to escape it.

When we open a physical door, it allows open access to anyone and anything that desires to come in. The same thing can happen spiritually. Doors to our heart, mind, and soul can be opened to different areas of oppression.

Write out Galatians 5:1 in the space below.

Living with oppression is similar to living under a "yoke of slavery." Oppression often comes into our lives with our agreement, whether we are aware of it or not. We may be tricked or deceived, or we may go into it with our eyes wide open, but it always involves a door being opened in our lives that should not have been opened.

Some people open doors to oppression through their choices and deliberate sin. Here are a few examples:

- In this week's story, Nancy made the choice to purge her food one night at her pastor's house, and it led to a mental and emotional prison of binging and purging for the next five years.
- Stan had made the choice to regularly watch horror films, but he found he couldn't sleep at night due to a constant paranoia that someone was breaking into his home. When Stan did sleep, he had persistent horrible nightmares.
- One night while in college, Tammy made the choice to look at a pornographic website. This decision opened the door to a 10-year pornography addiction that created massive oppression in Tammy's life.

At other times, oppression can come in through circumstances and situations we experience that are not within our control. Here are a few examples:

- From a young age, her parents physically and mentally abused Katie. As a result, she struggled with feeling out of control. Katie eventually turned to restricting food and other eating disorder behaviors to try and give herself a semblance of control over at least one aspect of her life.
- One night while Bill was walking through his neighborhood, a man attacked him and demanded his wallet while holding Bill at gunpoint. For years after the attack, Bill struggled with persistent nightmares and a great amount of fear when walking alone.
- As a child, his babysitter exposed Craig to inappropriate media and images. Then in his teen years and throughout his adulthood, Craig found himself regularly struggling with lustful thoughts and a desire to view pornography.

Regardless of who or how the door of oppression was opened in our lives, the good news is that we now have the choice to repent and close the door! If you have experienced the consequences of someone else opening that door in your life, our hearts break for your situation. But you now have the choice to get the help needed so that those experiences do not result in your living under oppression. It will not be an easy process, but we encourage you to seek professional help if you need to work through the effects of traumatic events from your life.

Take some time to consider your own life. Ask, "Father, is there an area of oppression that You would like me to be aware of and address this week? If so, what?" Write what He shows you below.

Just as doors to oppression may be opened in our lives because of unwise choices we (or others) have made, we also have the power, as followers of Christ, to shut those doors. If you are sitting on your couch and somebody walks into your house and loads up your TV and valuables, you wouldn't just sit there and let the intruder steal from you. You would say, "Wait a minute! What are you doing? Get back here with my stuff." You would call the police because you have a legal right to your possessions. Yet we so often let the enemy walk in and take whatever he wants. He steals our peace, torments us, cancels our joy, harms our relationships, and ruins our bodies. Oppression only stays with your permission. Throughout the rest of this week, we will discuss practical steps to get free and stay free from oppression.

> *Oppression only stays with your permission.*

Day 2: *Emotional Attachments*

Yesterday we defined oppression as "pressure" and anything that the enemy is able to bring into our lives through our choices or the choices of others in the form of habits, addictions, thought patterns, and even unhealthy relationships. Today we want to specifically discuss the area of unhealthy relationships, as this is an area that can negatively affect people without their awareness. While God created us to have relationships and connect with one another in healthy ways, some relationships become attached in ways outside of His design, forming an unhealthy or ungodly emotional attachment.

> *Relationships that position us to become more of who God created us to be and allow us to reciprocate this for others are the relationships we want to cultivate in our lives.*

Our lives overlap with others emotionally, sexually, and mentally. God designed us to be in healthy relationship and tied to others in ways that are life giving. Safe, two-way, honest, and committed marriages, friendships, parent-child relationships, and business/ministry partnerships are examples of healthy emotional attachments that bring tremendous blessing to our lives. Relationships that position us to become more of who God created us to be and allow us to reciprocate this for others are the relationships we want to cultivate in our lives. The easiest way to identify the health of our attachment is

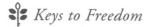

by examining the fruit of it. When healthy, the fruit of our lives intersecting with others will always reflect God's heart and purpose for connection.

However, sometimes we have the wrong influences in our lives (with or without our consent), and we can become connected in unhealthy ways through various means. Influences such as manipulation, intimidation, unhealthy emotional dependency, control and violation can all result in unhealthy attachments.

Another means in which unhealthy ties can be formed is through sexual interactions outside the boundaries of marriage (including sexual violations). While this is just one type of unhealthy emotional attachment, these ties are important to assess and address if you have not done so before, because they can have a lifelong negative influence on your life and your relationships.

Ultimately, unhealthy emotional attachments keep us bound in relationships in a way that is not healthy or life-giving for either person. Some specific signs of unhealthy emotional ties may include:

- Unhealthy care taking
- Lack of boundaries within the relationship
- Low self-esteem that affects decision making and boundary-setting
- People pleasing
- Dysfunctional communication
- Obsessions
- Overly dependent on one another
- Lack of additional outside relationships, isolation
- Constant sacrifice for the relationship
- Unequal give-and-take
- Lack of trust
- Guilt and manipulation used within the relationship for control

Often when these ties are present, individuals have a hard time separating themselves from the relationship—even when they want to and know that it's the right thing to do. There seems to be an invisible pull that makes it difficult to cut themselves free. Terms such as co-dependency, enmeshment, and lack of boundaries are one way to label some of the unhealthy emotional ties to which we are referring. Unhealthy emotional ties, particularly within family, are sometimes the hardest to identify because the ties and dynamics of the relationships have been in place for many years – perhaps generations.

Ellie used to talk with her mother every day but began to realize, after a friend pointed it out, that her mother was a negative influence on her with her guilt trips and emotional manipulation. Ellie struggled with knowing how to respond, as she did not want to hurt her mom's feelings by challenging these behaviors. Ellie prayed to break the unhealthy emotional attachment that she recognized in this relationship and asked the Lord what her next steps needed to be. She prayerfully decided to stop talking to her mom so frequently. Ellie knew that her mom needed to cultivate stronger friendships with other people and stop depending on her so much. Ellie also recruited some friends to hold her accountable to not talk with her mom more than she should. After a while, Ellie's mom did reach out to other people and sought some counseling. Over time, she and Ellie talked consistently again, but in a much healthier way. Change took place as a result of Ellie making the choice to address the unhealthy attachment through prayer and then work on setting and keeping boundaries. The result was worth it!

If you recognize any of the signs that we have identified regarding unhealthy emotional ties, we encourage you to start by addressing the emotional attachments that the Lord reveals to you in prayer and then setting boundaries as He leads. In some relationships, it may mean a clean break entirely, especially if it has been sinful and destructive. In others, it may mean redefining it, as Ellie did, by setting new boundaries and leaving room for the Lord to work in their life and in yours.

Ask the Lord, "Jesus, is there anyone in my life with whom I have an unhealthy emotional attachment? If so, who?" Write what He shows you below.

Breaking unhealthy emotional attachments is a simple, but powerful stance in the spirit that allows you to be free of relational ties that are not God's best for you. You have the authority and ability to choose who and what you are connected to. As you may have noticed in Ellie's story, she prayed, and then she acted. Breaking these unhealthy attachments is typically not just a prayer; it usually calls for conscious choices regarding the unhealthy parts of relationships in your life. If the Lord reveals people to you from your past who are no longer in your life (including people who may have abused you), pray to forgive them, and break the ties, and then ask for His direction in any further steps that He would have you take. A prayer to break emotional attachments is below:

Jesus, thank you for the freedom that is available to me through the power of Your Name and Your death on the cross. Thank You that You desire good, healthy relationships for me and empower me to make healthy choices. In the Name of Jesus, I choose to break the unhealthy emotional attachment(s) with _____. I release them from me and myself from them in the Name of Jesus. Amen.

Key 6: Choosing Freedom Over Oppression   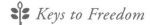 Keys to Freedom

Day 3: *Closing the Doors*

On Day 1 of this week, we discussed how the doors of oppression can be opened in our lives, but we ended the day by pointing out that as followers of Christ, we have the power and the choice to close those doors! Today we want to give you some practical steps to get free and stay free from any oppression that you might be experiencing, whether those doors were opened by your own choices or by the choices of others.

The first step to gaining freedom from oppression is to confess your sin and truly repent. Repentance literally means, "to turn around and go the other way." It's important to note that repentance is not a one-time event; it's a lifestyle. It happens over and over again for different areas of sin and struggle as we grow and mature. Through this process of confession and repentance, we may also need to address any lack of forgiveness toward ourselves or others who played a role in the oppression we are experiencing.

> *Repentance is not a one-time event; it's a lifestyle.*

Refer back to the area of oppression in your life that the Lord revealed to you on Day 1 of this week. For what areas of sin are you personally responsible? Are there any areas of unforgiveness that need to be addressed? Use the space below to confess and repent of those areas to the Lord.

After we genuinely confess the sin and walk away from it, we also set boundaries around whatever is within us that stirs up that temptation to sin and open the door to oppression. For example, if the area of oppression you repented of was lust, then you might cancel your cable TV and have an Internet accountability partner. You won't drive through sections of town where sexual sin is advertised and available. Or if your area of struggle is comparison, you might limit your social media consumption, where you're tempted to compare your life with the perception or portrayal of others.

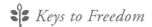

Are there any changes and/or boundaries that you need to add to your life to avoid temptation? If so, what are they? If you are unsure, pray and ask the Lord to highlight these things to you. Write out His response and your thoughts below.

There is a well-known scripture that says we are to resist the enemy. However, many people only quote the second half of the verse and fail to recognize the first half. James 4:7 says, "Submit yourself to God. Resist the devil, and he will flee from you".

According to this scripture, what must we do before we resist the devil?

The order is critical: submit to God first, then resist the devil, and he has to flee. What does submitting to God mean? It means aligning our lives with the way He has made possible for us to live. It starts with confessing and repenting of our sin, setting boundaries around our weak spots, and then submitting fully to the Lord. To submit to God means to shut the door on habitual sin and disobedience. Only then will resisting the enemy, in the way the Bible describes, actually work.

In the first full week of this study, we compared our lives to a tree with every part of our life attached to another part. Every part of our lives affects the others. If we decide to chop off the branch of a destructive habit or thought pattern, but hold on to known sin in other areas of our life, then we are simply deferring the damage from one branch to another and will keep growing poisonous fruit. For example, if you submit to God in the area of lust but do not address your fiery temper, unkind tongue, or unresolved hurts, the consequences are still destructive, not constructive.

Key 6: Choosing Freedom Over Oppression 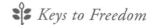 *Keys to Freedom*

Ask the Lord: "Jesus, are there any areas of my life where I have not fully submitted to Your ways? Are there any doors that I have not completely closed? If so, what are those areas? How would You like me to address them in prayer?" Write down what the Lord speaks to you and follow His leading in repentance, forgiveness, or any other direction He gives.

The bottom line is that submitting to God means submitting in all areas of life. When we do this as best we can, with a sincere commitment, the Holy Spirit empowers our choice and enables us to walk in ever-increasing freedom!

Day 4 - *Taking Authority*

Over the past couple of days, we have discussed the importance of confessing, repenting, and setting necessary boundaries in your life. Once you have taken these steps, you have the legal right to declare your authority over the enemy and command oppression to go in Jesus' Name. This authority does not come from the power of our personality or will, our cleverness, or resolve. It comes through the power of Christ! Jesus purchased our freedom and legally defeated Satan when He was resurrected and triumphed over sin and death after hanging on the cross and shedding His blood.

What does Colossians 2:15 say that Jesus did to the enemy's "principalities and powers"?

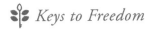

Key 6: Choosing Freedom Over Oppression

Because of the finished work of Jesus at the cross, Satan no longer has legal authority in the lives of God's children. However, he does have as much power and influence in our lives as we allow him to have. As a son or daughter of God, you choose how much oppression you are willing to allow into your life. Our victory has been won, but we must use our God-given authority as believers to enforce the enemy's defeat.

> *The enemy does have as much power and influence in our lives as we allow him to have.*

If you pray in Jesus' Name, Satan is forced to leave. He may try to come back, but stand firm knowing that Satan has nothing in comparison to the authority you have through Jesus. Pray out loud, and command the enemy to get out of your life; then get ready for freedom!

Is it possible that we will make the choice to close a door of oppression in our lives and then re-open that door at some point down the road? Of course. We are not talking about perfection, rather, a sincere commitment to obey wholeheartedly. Remember that God will always be there to meet you where you are. He is not there to condemn you or shame you. You simply use these same tools of confession, repentance, and submission to close those doors of oppression again.

Remember the truths of God's Word and press on toward the freedom Jesus died to give you. Philippians 3:12–14 says, "I'm not saying that I have this all together, that I have it made. But I am well on my way, reaching out for Christ, who has so wondrously reached out for me. Friends, don't get me wrong: By no means do I count myself an expert in all of this, but I've got my eye on the goal, where God is beckoning us onward—to Jesus. I'm off and running, and I'm not turning back" (MSG).

Remember that Satan has been defeated. Revelation 20:10 says that Satan will be thrown into a lake of burning sulfur, where he "will be tormented day and night forever and ever." So when he comes to remind you of your past, remind him of his future!

God loves you and does not want you to live in the nightmare and heartache of oppression any longer! He hears the cry of your heart and will set you free from bondage. Below is an example of a prayer to take authority over oppression. As we said before, you are not praying and asking the Lord to take authority for you. You are standing in the authority that Jesus already purchased on the cross and gave to you when you committed your life to Him. Look back to any areas that the Lord revealed to you this week and address those now.

> ***Jesus, thank you that Satan has already been defeated in my life. I use the authority You have given me, submit myself to You, and command _____ (area(s) of oppression) to leave me. I close the door to _____ (area(s) of oppression) now in Jesus' Name. I***

Key 6: Choosing Freedom Over Oppression

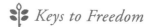 Keys to Freedom

choose to walk in freedom from this sin and will not give in to its temptations. Satan has no power over my life, and I surrender all my thoughts, attitudes, and actions to You alone. I will be ready when the enemy tries to lead me away from Your will. I choose to stand firm in the promises You give me in Your Word. In Jesus' Name, Amen.

If there are any other areas of your life not submitted to God that you identify in the future, you can always go back to the principles we've discussed over the past couple of days and apply them again!

Close today's study by writing Psalm 9:9–10 in your own words in the space below. Then take a few moments to meditate on the truth of this scripture, and thank God for being your refuge.

Day 5: *Identifying the Enemy's Voice*

Over the past two days of study, we have given you some practical keys for finding freedom from oppression. Today we want to talk about an important key for *staying* free from oppression.

As we mentioned on Day 1 of this week, some people open the door to various kinds of oppression through their choices and deliberate sin. Others fall into it unsuspectingly. We talked about how oppression often comes into our lives with our agreement. We may be tricked or deceived, or we may go into it with our eyes wide open, but it often involves opening a door we should not have opened. The key to staying free from oppression, then, is making sure that the doors of oppression stay closed in our lives. One way to do is this is to become very skilled in identifying the voice of the enemy.

Study Guide

What does Ephesians 4:27 warn us about giving to the enemy?

The enemy is always hoping to get a foothold in our lives. He is always trying to entice us into sin and oppression. If we have not been trained to know the difference between God's voice and the enemy's voice, we are susceptible to falling for his trickery and deceit. Thankfully, the Lord is faithful to speak to us!

On Day 4 of the first full week of study "Setting the Stage" we discussed a few of the main ways that we can confirm what the Lord is speaking to us. Take a moment to review those, and write them below. Then circle some of the ways the Lord has confirmed what He has spoken to you throughout this study.

Is there anything else that you have learned about the way the Lord confirms what He reveals to us? Write your thoughts below.

Remember that above all, God's voice and His Word always line up. If what you receive does not line up with truth from the Bible, you will know that it is not from God. The enemy's words are often centered on our personal gratification and do not line up with our circumstances or the counsel that godly people are giving to us.

Another way we can discern God's voice from the enemy's voice is by examining our own emotional response. When you experience fear, worry, condemnation, or confusion, you can be assured that it is from the enemy. When what you hear or feel leads to reassurance, peace, encouragement, comfort and revelation, you know that it is the Holy Spirit.

When you experience fear, worry, condemnation, or confusion, you can be assured that it is from the enemy.

The Bible tells us that it's not difficult for a sincere follower of Christ to distinguish between the Holy Spirit's voice and the enemy's. It will begin to come naturally as you continue to spend time with God and in His Word.

Read John 10:3–4. In verse 4, why does it say that the sheep follow the shepherd?

Sheep learn and know their shepherd's voice. The prophet Isaiah said, "Whether you turn to the right or to the left, your ears will hear a voice behind you saying, "This is the way; walk in it" (Isa. 30:21). Jesus promised that "…the Counselor, the Holy Spirit, whom the Father will send in My name, will teach you everything and remind you of all that I told you" (John 14:26).

At times, the enemy may attempt to interject his lies and confusion into our lives as a means of keeping us stuck and unsure of how we should move forward. You may have experienced this at one point or another in your life or even during the course of this study. The enemy watches for moments to come in when we are tired, sick, or weak. He will often attempt to speak right before we are about to make a stand in our authority to remove him. The wonderful thing is that the voice of the Lord and the voice of the enemy are very, very different.

Can you think of a time in your life when you felt that the enemy was speaking to you? Were you able to recognize any of the various types of fruit that come when he speaks, such as fear or condemnation? If so, what? Explain below.

If you choose to follow the Lord's voice, the Holy Spirit will wonderfully encourage and enable you to walk that way. If you choose the voice of self-gratification, the enemy will be there egging you on. Every choice is empowered by either God or the enemy. It all starts with you discerning and then choosing which voice you will follow. As you grow in your ability to discern God's voice from the enemy's voice, you will be able to keep the doors of oppression closed in your life and walk in ever-increasing freedom!

JOURNAL

What did God speak or show to you throughout the week?

Don't forget to share what God is doing in your life or any valuable insights you have received. And be sure to use the #KeystoFreedom hashtag!

Key 7
Maintaining Lifelong Freedom

Day 1: *The Four Stay-Ins*

This study has described and taught you the keys to freedom that God has made available to us all through a relationship with Jesus Christ. For over three decades, we have seen these keys bring transformation in the lives of thousands. However, the power of a key is in its actual use. We have learned that living a life of freedom has always come to those who did not just use these keys to be free from their past but those who continued to use them to take hold of their future. Today we will look at some of the key lifestyle choices that have helped our Mercy girls and many other people maintain freedom for life. We refer to these lifestyle choices as "The Four Stay-ins".

Stay in Prayer

At this point in the study, we hope you have experienced how prayer is the essence of your personal relationship with God. It is to your spiritual life what breathing is to your physical life. It is turning your attention to your ultimate Source and talking with Him throughout the day, acknowledging Him in all your ways, and giving Him space to have a voice into your life as a son or daughter.

> *Prayer is to your spiritual life what breathing is to your physical life.*

Read Ephesians 6:18 and Philippians 4:6–7. What do these scriptures tell you about staying in prayer?

Stay in the Word

One of the most powerful ways for us to interact with God is through the Bible. Through His Word, God reveals to us His heart, directs us, and speaks to our life situations and our true identity as His sons and daughters.

In Key 2: Renewing the Mind, we talked about the importance of meditating on the Word. For review, what does Jesus say the truth (the Word) will do for us in John 8:31–32?

Remember, though, it's not simply the truth that sets you free; it's the truth you know that sets you free. There is no freedom apart from conforming your life to the Word of God (see Psalm 119:9). Why? Because God's Word "is alive and active. Sharper than any double-edged sword, it penetrates even to dividing soul and spirit, joints and marrow; it judges the thoughts and attitudes of the heart." (Heb. 4:12). In other words, the Word of God powerfully works in us to sustain our freedom in Christ; it discerns and exposes lies so that we can make decisions for our lives that are in line with His Word.

Stay in Fellowship

Scripture tells us that our lives will flourish when we choose to be planted in the house of the Lord (see Psalm 92:13), which is His church, His people, and His body. God's global church has many different expressions, but God's heart is that each of us finds a place to call home and bloom where we are planted. Whether it is in a gathering of thousands or a small group of people meeting in someone's home, the Church is your spiritual family.

What does Hebrews 10:24-25 tell us to do?

If your experience of the local church has been difficult or painful, make sure you go back to Key 3: Healing Life's Hurts, and walk through your experiences, using the keys you now have. God is with you, and His desire is that you find connection within the family that He has given to you. Ask Him to help you find the place where He is planting you. Keep in mind that while no church is perfect, and no group of people is without fault, having a home and a family of believers around you is an important part of walking out your freedom.

Stay in Accountability

Read Proverbs 27:17. What does this scripture mean to you? Do you have relationships in your life that "sharpen" you? If so, who?

We are meant to be in relationship with people who we sharpen and who sharpen us. It is also wise to have a couple of people with whom you fellowship to be aware of potential areas of struggle and difficulty you may be currently working to overcome. If you don't already have accountability or mentor relationships in your life, you may be able to establish them with people who are already in your life or possibly in your small group. Look for mature Christians who have a heart for people and are willing to be honest, to pray, and to ask you the hard questions when necessary. People can't sharpen you if they don't know what is happening in your life. This also positions you to have additional prayer support as you walk out different seasons of growth, healing, and freedom.

Are you willing to make some intentional changes in your daily life to sustain your freedom? If so, God will help you all the way. Does this mean you should expect perfection from yourself? Of course not! When a baby learns to walk, he is not scolded when he falls. His parents are excited to see him learning and growing. God looks at you with great joy as you do your best to walk in Him. When you fall, He simply picks you up and sends you on your way to try again. The key is to be faithful and relentlessly come back to the path of freedom.

Review each of The Four Stay-ins that we discussed today. What are three practical changes you want to make in your life to help you walk in ongoing freedom through these principles? Write them below and make a heart commitment to implement them right away.

Day 2: *Dressed for the Process*

If you've ever taken a trip overseas, you know that it often includes multiple flights, layovers, and car rides to get from one destination to the next. The journey can be long and exhausting. Wouldn't it be great if we could just reach our final destination without having to go through the process to get there?

In the Introduction of this book, Nancy Alcorn shared that this study is not a magic wand to wave over your struggles and adversities. Our God is a God of process. As much as we desire for God to simply heal us and set us free in an instant, we are not called to be passive recipients of His power. Instead, we are called and invited to partner with Him in a powerful process.

The steps and principles outlined in this study are the process for freedom and wholeness that God has given to us through His Word. It may seem counterintuitive to you that things like forgiveness and vulnerability will lead to your freedom, but this is where we must trust that God knows what He is doing. He is the "specialist" on your heart, and He knows the exact process you must take to experience lasting change and breakthrough.

It's important to know that God doesn't choose process as some sort of punishment. He's not trying to figure out a way to make things difficult for us. God knows that one of the most important purposes of process is that persistent obedience is grown through it. This study has given you principles of freedom that must be put into regular practice in the days, weeks, and years to come. Don't be discouraged if you are wrapping up this study but still don't feel like you have experienced your breakthrough. If you make the choice to be persistent in your obedience to the biblical principles that you have learned, your breakthrough will come!

The good news is that God has promised to empower you through the process. All Christians have access to the same power that raised Christ from the dead, but so many never put it to use. It does you no good to have the power and authority of the Holy Spirit but never use it. We must learn how to apply the freedom that Jesus died for us to have! It is an ongoing choice that God continually empowers.

If it has not already become clear to you, we are in a war. Each one of us is in a daily fight for our hearts and our lives, whether or not we are aware of it. We have an enemy. And he is working day and night to steal, kill and destroy our lives. Throughout this study, you may have become even more keenly aware at how the enemy has strategized against your own life and freedom. However, we have also learned that because we belong to Christ, the enemy doesn't have the final authority in our lives! He is a defeated foe, and 1 John 4:4 reminds us that "he who is in [us] is greater than he who is in the world."

Key 7: Maintaining Lifelong Freedom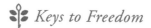

So how do we safeguard ourselves as we continue to walk out the process? In Ephesians 6, we read about the armor of God that is available to all of His children. We have a choice every day as to whether or not we will pick up the armor of God and put it on.

What does 2 Corinthians 10:4 say about the weapons God gives us to use?

Read Ephesians 6:11-18. What reason does verse 11 give for putting on the armor?

Next to each of the pieces of armor listed below, write the corresponding spiritual attribute from the passage, and then ask God to show you why that attribute is so important to your daily walking in freedom. Ask the Holy Spirit to highlight things for you that perhaps you have never noticed in this passage of Scripture.

Belt -

Breastplate -

Shoes -

Shield -

Helmet -

Sword -

Study Guide | 117

Ask, "Lord, how can I practically pick up Your armor every day as I continue walking forward into new levels of freedom?" Write what He shows you below.

Day 3: *It's All in the Seed*

Before you create something, you first determine its purpose. So before God designed you, He already knew the destiny and purpose that He was creating you to fulfill.

Darcy, a friend of Mercy, shares a powerful analogy of the purpose God has for our lives in the example of a seed. All seeds hold within them everything that is needed for the seed to fully grow into the purpose and plan that was originally intended for it. For example, everything needed for an apple tree is in the seed for that tree, such as the bark, branches, root system, and apples (including the color and particular taste). The seed does not lack anything it needs to become what it was originally intended to be.

> *God already put inside of us what we need to fulfill the purposes that He has planned for us.*

Fish don't have to go to swim school. Birds don't have to go to flight school. They already have inside of them what they need. Likewise, God already put inside of us what we need to fulfill the purposes that He has planned for us. We each carry seeds of purpose, destiny, and identity that have been within us since creation.

Read Ephesians 2:10. When does it say God planned the good works for us to do?

Key 7: Maintaining Lifelong Freedom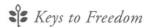

If you have ever gardened, you know that there are certain external factors, such as sunlight, water, healthy soil, and tending hands that need to be in place in order for a seed to germinate and eventually grow into the final product it holds within. It is a process, and sometimes those necessary factors may or may not be in place. If the right external factors are in place, the seed is positioned to grow and flourish as it was intended. If the seed is neglected or comes into contact with harmful factors, such as harsh weather or toxins in the environment, the seed will struggle to become all that it was intended to be. However, this does not change the fact that the seed still holds everything it needs to flourish.

There are purposes for our lives that are in seed form within each of us. The seeds were planted there by the Creator of our lives who has a vision for each of us as His children. However, much like the seed that hit harsh weather and toxins in the environment, our lives can often experience similar things through hurt, abuse, and disappointments. When that happens, the seeds of destiny and purpose within us may begin to lie dormant. We may begin moving away from the original design for our lives as we attempt to survive the difficulties we face. The poison that might go into a tree was never part of God's purpose for that tree. Likewise, the hurtful experiences of your life and the lies that the world has thrown at you have nothing to do with your original God-design.

There is a story about a basket of wheat seeds that has been sitting in one of the pyramids in Egypt for 4,000 years. A tourist asked their guide if anyone had ever tried to plant one of the seeds. The tour guide affirmed that someone had once taken a few of the seeds and planted them. Even though the seeds had been lying dormant for 4,000 years in the desert of Egypt, they grew into healthy stalks of wheat once they were planted and cared for!

What does this show us about the seeds that are within us? If a seed is placed in the wrong environment, it won't grow. But it is never too late! You may have faced a lot of darkness, isolation, and difficulty in your life, but the seeds of destiny within you are still there. They simply need to be planted in the right environment. In John 15:5, Jesus said, "I am the vine; you are the branches. Those who remain in me, and I in them, will produce much fruit. For apart from me you can do nothing." He wants to restore and nourish the seeds that He has placed in our lives. We simply have to make the choice to stay connected to Him so that we are positioned to be fruitful as He originally purposed us to be.

Is this concept of seeds new to you? What are your initial thoughts about the seeds of destiny and purpose that you carry?

Keys to Freedom Key 7: Maintaining Lifelong Freedom

How have the seeds in your life been cultivated? List some of the positive and negative factors that have affected them.

As you wrap up today, take a moment to tell the Lord how it makes you feel that He has placed seeds of destiny and purpose into your life. Ask Him to start stirring up vision and passion for any seeds that may have been lying dormant or unidentified.

Day 4: *Know, Sow, and then Grow*

In order to know what you're growing, you must first identify the kind of seed with which you are working. As mentioned yesterday, all of us have seeds of destiny and purpose that the Lord placed inside of us. Some of those seeds may have started to sprout up in our lives while others may be lying dormant and unidentified. As simple as it may sound, if you want to grow an apple tree, you need to be sure you are working with apple seeds. You must take the time to read the package and identify the seeds. It is the same with the seeds that have been planted in our lives. We need to take the time to identify what they hold in order to pursue the fullness they carry in our lives.

> *The seeds of destiny and purpose that God places inside of us are unique, individual and special.*

The seeds of destiny and purpose that God places inside of us are unique, individual, and special. Just as there are no two snowflakes that are the

Key 7: Maintaining Lifelong Freedom 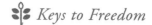 Keys to Freedom

same, the seeds within each of our lives are all unique as well. When identifying what the seeds in our lives hold, it is important to pay attention to a few things:

Passion – The things that stir passion in you are often a cue to some of the things that your unique seeds carry. You may find that your heart seems to beat quickly when you do certain things like serving other people or painting a picture or teaching little children. Or you might notice that same stirring in your heart when you witness a youth pastor ministering to students, a craftsman creating things with their hands or a parent loving on their children. Pay attention to those moments when your heart stirs!

What are some things you are most passionate about doing? What makes your heart stir? Write your thoughts in the "Passion" seed below.

Righteous Anger –The things that stir up a righteous anger inside of you may be a cue to some of the areas of impact that the Lord has placed in your seeds. This impact may come through giving of your time, resources, or talents to the areas where you desire to see change.

What injustices, difficulties, or problems make you angry or lay heavy on your heart? Child abuse, poverty, illiteracy, homelessness? Write your thoughts in the "Anger" seed below.

Dreams – Whether you are aware of them or not, there are God-sized dreams attached to the seeds of destiny that He has placed in your life. Ephesians 3:20 reminds us that God is able to do immeasurably more than all we ask or imagine according to His power that is at work within us. That scripture can be both exhilarating and scary! His dreams for us are always immeasurably more amazing and wonderful than what we can even dare to dream.

What are the dreams that God has placed in your heart? Are there any dreams you had as a child before life and responsibility and hurts came on the scene? Write your thoughts in the "Dreams" seed below.

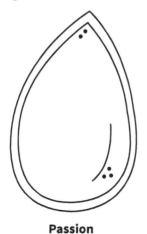
Passion

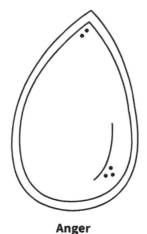
Anger

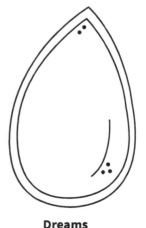
Dreams

Ask the Lord, "Is there anything specific in the areas of passion, anger, or dreams that you want to highlight for me today? Are there any other things that my seeds hold that You would like to reveal? If so, what?" Write what He shows you below.

We hope you have received some new revelation about what God has placed inside of you. It is now time to ask the Lord to restore life and purpose to any of those seeds in your life that need to be cultivated. This can be done through the simple prayer below. Tomorrow we will discuss your next steps for walking in purpose and destiny! Pray this prayer as you wrap up your time today:

Jesus, thank You for placing individual and unique seeds of purpose and destiny in my life. I am excited to begin to see what these seeds hold. I choose to believe that no matter what I have experienced or walked through, it is never too late for You to restore life and health to those seeds. I ask You to breathe Your living breath onto the seeds in my life and to begin to show me how to partner with You in moving forward in all that You have for me. I thank You that the past is behind me and that a beautiful and full destiny awaits ahead, in Jesus' Name. Amen.

Whatever you have identified as potential seed will require a lot of cultivating to become planted and bear fruit. Our suggestion is to become deliberate and very practical about growing your seed.

Close today by asking the Lord, "What specific steps would You have me take in cultivating the seeds of purpose You have placed in my life? Are there areas of experience or qualification that I can pursue? Perhaps read a book, take a class, volunteer, connect with a certain person/mentor, or begin giving to an organization?"

Key 7: Maintaining Lifelong Freedom

Day 5: *Next Steps*

The last two days have been spent discussing the seeds of destiny and purpose that God placed in your life and identifying what they hold. Today we want to bring everything together and focus on your next steps, not only in regards to what the Lord has shown you this week, but also in how you will put to work the tools you have learned throughout the course of this study.

As we have discussed many times, healing and wholeness is a process that continues throughout your lifetime. We pray that these past few weeks have equipped you with new revelation, heart connection with the Lord, and tools to use in your freedom journey, but the journey has just begun for many of you! At this point, you may feel excited about the future or you may feel overwhelmed. We want to encourage you to remember that the work you have done, and will continue to do, is truly a process.

2 Corinthians 3:18 says, "But we all, with unveiled face, beholding as in a mirror the glory of the Lord, are being transformed into the same image from glory to glory..." (NASB). The journey to freedom is a process of moving from strength to strength and glory to glory. We hope you see some great changes in your life and in your heart from where you were when you started this study. But just imagine how different you will be in another month, or six months, or a year, as you choose to continue to put the tools and principles you've learned in this study to work!

> *The journey to freedom is a process of moving from strength to strength and glory to glory.*

It's now time to seek the Lord for your next steps by praying through the questions below.

"Lord, what are some of the highlights from this *Keys to Freedom* study experience for which You are most proud of me and excited about as I move forward?"

Study Guide | 123

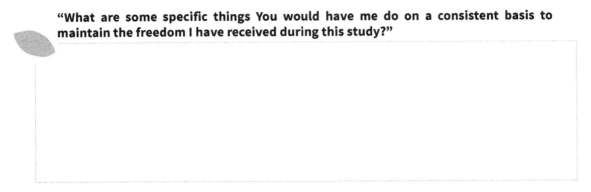

"What are some specific things You would have me do on a consistent basis to maintain the freedom I have received during this study?"

On Day 3 of this week, we discussed how everything needed for an apple tree is in the seed for that tree, such as the bark, branches, root system, and apples. However, there is another important thing inside the seeds of an apple tree that we did not mention: more trees! When God creates something, He puts a seed inside for that thing to multiply. The seed will reproduce after its own kind. God has placed something inside of you to multiply, and the greatest calling of your life is to join Him in multiplying His peace, love, joy, and freedom to a lost and hurting world!

The first commandment that God gave to mankind in Genesis 1 was, "Be fruitful and multiply." The thing about fruit on trees is that it's not there to benefit the tree, but to benefit other people. You will pass on to others whatever it is that you carry. So, you see, this journey to freedom was never solely about you. It finds its completion when it not only transforms your life, but when the lives of others are impacted by the hope and joy and freedom in which you are now living. There are people on the other side of this journey whose lives will be forever impacted by your obedience to pursue freedom and wholeness. So the question we leave you with is: "Who's on the other side of your obedience?"

We pray that you will make the choice to continue this journey, so that you will not only walk in the fullness you were created to experience, but so that many others will experience it as freedom multiplies in and through you!

Key 7: Maintaining Lifelong Freedom 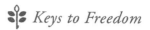 Keys to Freedom

JOURNAL

What did God speak or show to you throughout the week?

Don't forget to share what God is doing in your life or any valuable insights you have received.
And be sure to use the #KeystoFreedom hashtag!

 *Keys to Freedom*

Conclusion

Jesus has won the victory and given you the power to walk in life and peace! We hope that the keys to freedom you have learned and experienced have powerfully connected you to God's heart, your true identity in Him, and the vision and plan that He has for you! Our prayer is that you are now equipped to continue your own personal healing journey and to give the keys that you learned during this time to others as well.

There is a life of victory that is ahead of you, and not just for you but also for your children, your grandchildren, and anyone else you influence. Your victory is designed to grow and impact everyone around you. You are becoming a shining example of God's grace in the midst of whatever situation you are in. If you stumble, remember that the key to success is to trust in the grace of God and return to the road of freedom no matter how many times you fall.

Revelation 12:11 states that we overcome by the blood of the Lamb and by the word of our testimony. We encourage you to recognize that you have started the process of overcoming during this study, and as you keep putting your keys to work and telling the story of what God has done, you will continue to overcome at new levels in the days to come!

The last thing for you to do in this study is to make a formal commitment to living in freedom. On the next page, you will find a list of the important principles and life-transforming truths we have talked about in this study. Commit to living out these keys to freedom for the rest of your life. Also, share your commitment with at least one other person who can encourage you and cheer you on as you continue to walk this journey.

We would love to hear your testimonies of how God used this study to help you in this season of your life. Feel free to e-mail us at Outreach@MercyMultiplied.com, so we can rejoice with you and partner with you in prayer.

We firmly believe in the keys and principles outlined in this study because we have seen them work time and time again. At Mercy, we plan to expand our reach and help others outside our walls realize this kind of lasting freedom. We are going to multiply our efforts and watch God multiply His freedom. Visit www.MercyMultiplied.com for more resources and to see how you can get involved in helping others find healing and freedom and change their lives!

Commitment to Freedom

As God's son or daughter walking in FREEDOM and living in the position of authority that is mine as His child, I receive the truth that …

- Transformation takes total commitment and connection to Christ. I can't simply offer part of my heart and life to God and expect to walk in freedom.

- Renewing my mind is an active, ongoing process that leads to greater freedom as I commit to replacing untrue thoughts with truth from God's Word.

- When I acknowledge the hurts I have experienced and invite the Lord to give me His perspective, I allow God to heal me and bring new levels of freedom and peace.

- Forgiveness is a vital key to living in freedom. It is a choice of obedience, not a feeling, but my feelings will follow when I make the sincere commitment to forgive.

- Breaking generational patterns comes by identifying and taking authority over them based on my authority as a follower of Jesus.

- God has given me the power to overcome oppression in my life as I submit to Him and close the door on choices that result in a loss of freedom.

- Walking in freedom for a lifetime is a process, and I commit to staying in prayer, staying in the Word, and staying in fellowship and accountability with other strong believers. I commit to putting on the armor of God every day and pursuing the destiny and calling that He has on my life.

I am a new creation in Christ. The old is gone, and I am made new. I commit to these keys to freedom for the rest of my life and know that freedom is mine!

_____   _____
Signed   **Date**

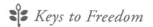

Appendix A

"Who I Am In Christ"

Practice saying these verses out loud to help renew your mind with God's Word about your identity in Christ:

- I am a child of God: "To all who believed him and accepted him, he gave the right to become children of God" (John 1:12, NLT).
- I am the light of the world: "You are the light of the world—like a city on a hilltop that cannot be hidden" (Matt. 5:14, NLT).
- I am a joint heir with Christ: "Since we are his children, we are his heirs. In fact, together with Christ we are heirs of God's glory" (Rom. 8:17, NLT).
- I am a temple, a dwelling place of God: "Don't you realize that your body is the temple of the Holy Spirit, who lives in you and was given to you by God?" (1 Cor. 6:19, NLT).
- I am a new creation: "Anyone who belongs to Christ has become a new person. The old life is gone; a new life has begun!" (2 Cor. 5:17, NLT).
- I am righteous and holy: "Put on your new nature, created to be like God—truly righteous and holy" (Eph. 4:24, NLT).
- I am a threat to the devil: "I have given you authority to trample on snakes and scorpions and to overcome all the power of the enemy; nothing will harm you" (Luke 10:19).
- I am free from condemnation: "There is no condemnation for those who belong to Christ Jesus" (Rom. 8:1, NLT).
- I may approach God with confidence: "Because of Christ and our faith in him, we can now come boldly and confidently into God's presence" (Eph. 3:12, NLT).
- I am complete in Christ: "You also are complete through your union with Christ, who is the head over every ruler and authority" (Col. 2:10, NLT).
- I have been redeemed and forgiven from all of my sins: "He has rescued us from the kingdom of darkness and transferred us into the Kingdom of his dear Son, who purchased our freedom and forgave our sins" (Col. 1:13–14, NLT).
- I am of the light and no longer belong to the darkness: "You are all children of the light and children of the day. We do not belong to the night or to the darkness" (1 Thess. 5:5).
- I am chosen: "For you are a people holy to the Lord your God. The Lord your God has chosen you out of all the peoples on the face of the earth to be his people, his treasured possession" (Deut. 7:6).
- I am beautiful and flawless: "You are altogether beautiful, my darling; there is no flaw in you" (Song of Sol. 4:7).

- I have peace: "The Lord gives strength to his people; the Lord blesses his people with peace" (Ps. 29:11).
- I am accepted: "Accept one another, then, just as Christ accepted you, in order to bring praise to God" (Rom. 15:7).
- I am more than a conqueror: "In all these things we are more than conquerors through him who loved us" (Rom. 8:37).
- I am confident and fearless: "For God has not given us a spirit of fear and timidity, but of power, love, and self-discipline" (2 Tim. 1:7, NLT).
- I am treasured: "For you are a people holy to the Lord your God. The Lord your God has chosen you out of all the peoples on the face of the earth to be his people, his treasured possession" (Deut. 7:6).
- I am worthy of His love: "They will walk with me, dressed in white, for they are worthy" (Rev. 3:4).
- I am a delight to God: "For the Lord takes delight in his people" (Ps. 149:4).
- I am secure: "Let the beloved of the Lord rest secure in him, for he shields him all day long, and the one the Lord loves rests between his shoulders" (Deut. 33:12).
- I am loved unconditionally: "Neither height nor depth, nor anything else in all creation, will be able to separate us from the love of God that is in Christ Jesus our Lord" (Rom. 8:39).
- I am gifted: "We have different gifts, according to the grace given to each of us" (Rom. 12:6).
- I am created in the image of God: "God created human beings in his own image" (Gen. 1:27, NLT).
- I am a citizen of heaven: "But we are citizens of heaven, where the Lord Jesus Christ lives. And we are eagerly waiting for him to return as our Savior" (Phil. 3:20, NLT).

Appendix B
Faulty Beliefs and Freedom Facts

If you find yourself wrestling with any of the following faulty beliefs, renew your mind by meditating on the Freedom facts and related truths from Scripture.

Faulty Belief: I am alone, and no one really cares how I feel or what I do.
Freedom Fact: God is always with me. He sees how I feel, and He comforts me.
Truth of Scripture: "Cast all your anxiety on him because he cares for you" (1 Pet. 5:7). "The Lord himself goes before you and will be with you; he will never leave you nor forsake you. Do not be afraid; do not be discouraged" (Deut. 31:8).

Faulty Belief: I'm not worth much. I don't deserve anything good.
Freedom Fact: I have been blessed with every spiritual blessing. Because I am a child of God, I have an eternal inheritance in heaven.
Truth of Scripture: "Now we live with great expectation, and we have a priceless inheritance—an inheritance that is kept in heaven for you, pure and undefiled, beyond the reach of change and decay" (1 Pet. 1:3–4, NLT). "All praise to God, the Father of our Lord Jesus Christ, who has blessed us with every spiritual blessing in the heavenly realms because we are united with Christ" (Eph. 1:3, NLT).

Faulty Belief: My looks don't measure up to what the world says is attractive. I am ugly.
Freedom Fact: All of God's works are great and wonderful, and that includes me! I am created in the image of God Himself, and He has created me beautifully.
Truth of Scripture: "For you created my inmost being; you knit me together in my mother's womb. I praise you because I am fearfully and wonderfully made; your works are wonderful, I know that full well" (Ps. 139:13–14). "He has made everything beautiful in its time" (Eccles. 3:11). "God created human beings in his own image" (Gen. 1:27, NLT).

Faulty Belief: Because I have lived a lie, I am unable to speak truth.
Freedom Fact: I can speak truth because the Spirit of God leads me. There is freedom in living an honest life.
Truth of Scripture: "When He, the Spirit of truth, comes, he will guide you into all the truth. He will not speak on his own; he will speak only what he hears, and he will tell you what is yet to come" (John 16:13). "Then you will know the truth, and the truth will set you free" (John 8:32).

Faulty Belief: God is going to have a hard time forgiving me for the things I have done and wrong choices I have made that hurt people.

Freedom Fact: God delights to show grace. His forgiveness is endless, and His mercies are new every morning.

Truth of Scripture: "Who is a God like you, who pardons sin and forgives the transgression of the remnant of his inheritance? You do not stay angry forever but delight to show mercy" (Mic. 7:18). "If we confess our sins, he is faithful and just and will forgive us our sins and purify us from all unrighteousness" (1 John 1:9).

Faulty Belief: I will only be satisfied and happy in life if I succeed in my career. My worth is in my achievements.

Freedom Fact: My value and my worth do not come from temporary worldly success or achievement, but they come from the fact that I am a child of the King and am fully loved and treasured by Him.

Truth of Scripture: "What is the price of two sparrows—one copper coin? But not a single sparrow can fall to the ground without your Father knowing it. And the very hairs on your head are all numbered. So don't be afraid; you are more valuable to God than a whole flock of sparrows" (Matt. 10:29–31). "He has made everything beautiful in its time" (Eccles. 3:11). "For you are a people holy to the Lord your God. The Lord your God has chosen you out of all the peoples on the face of the earth to be his people, his treasured possession" (Deut. 7:6).

Faulty Belief: Not even God could love me after what I have been through.

Freedom Fact: God loves me always, and nothing can separate me from His unfailing love. I choose to repent and turn to God.

Truth of Scripture: "I have loved you with an everlasting love; I have drawn you with unfailing kindness" (Jer. 31:3). "For I am convinced that neither death nor life, neither angels nor demons, neither the present nor the future, nor any powers, neither height nor depth, nor anything else in all creation, will be able to separate us from the love of God that is in Christ Jesus our Lord" (Rom. 8:38–39).

Faulty Belief: I will never amount to anything because I was used and abused.

Freedom Fact: I am more than a conqueror through Christ and have overcome the shame of my past. God has an amazing plan and purpose for my life, and He will give me the strength I need as I press toward it.

Truth of Scripture: "Forgetting what is behind and straining toward what is ahead, I press on toward the goal to win the prize for which God has called me heavenward in Christ Jesus" (Phil. 3:13–14). "But you belong to God, my dear children. You have already won a victory over those people, because the Spirit who lives in you is greater than the spirit who lives in the world" (1 John 4:4, NLT). "For I know the plans I have for you," declares the Lord, "plans to prosper you and not to harm you, plans to give you hope and a future" (Jer. 29:11).

Faulty Belief: I will always be sad and depressed.

Freedom Fact: My inheritance, as a child of God, is joy and hope. He can heal my pain, lift my burdens, and replace my mourning with joy.

Truth of Scripture: "Sing for joy, O heavens! Rejoice, O earth! Burst into song, O mountains! For the Lord has comforted his people and will have compassion on them in their suffering." (Matt. 10:29–31). "He has made everything beautiful in its time" (Eccles. 3:11). "For the kingdom of God is not a matter of eating and drinking, but of righteousness, peace, and joy in the Holy Spirit…" (Deut. 7:6). "The Spirit of the Sovereign Lord is on me, because the Lord has anointed me to proclaim good news to the poor. He has sent me to bind up the brokenhearted, to proclaim freedom for the captives and release from darkness for the prisoners, to proclaim the year of the Lord's favor and the day of vengeance of our God, to comfort all who mourn, and provide for those who grieve in Zion—to bestow on them a crown of beauty instead of ashes, the oil of joy instead of mourning, and a garment of praise instead of a spirit of despair" (Is. 61:1–3).

Faulty Belief: If I let down my guard, something bad will happen to my children.

Freedom Fact: God is my protector and is with me wherever I go. I will be confident because God will take care of me.

Truth of Scripture: "For God has not given us a spirit of fear and timidity, but of power, love, and self-discipline" (2 Tim. 1:7, NLT). "For the Lord your God is living among you. He is a mighty savior. He will take delight in you with gladness. With his love, he will calm all your fears" (Zeph. 3:17, NLT). "For our present troubles are small and won't last very long. Yet they produce for us a glory that vastly outweighs them and will last forever!" (2 Cor. 4:17, NLT).

Faulty Belief: There is no hope for me to experience God's purpose and plan for my life because of what has happened to me and because of the choices I have made.

Freedom Fact: I am a child of God, and nothing can change that! He has great plans for my life and is faithful to continue the good work He started in me.

Truth of Scripture: "For I know the plans I have for you," says the Lord. "They are plans for good and not for disaster, to give you a future and a hope" (Jer. 29:11, NLT). "And I am certain that God, who began the good work within you, will continue his work until it is finally finished on the day when Christ Jesus returns" (Phil. 1:6, NLT). "May the God of hope fill you with all joy and peace as you trust in him, so that you may overflow with hope by the power of the Holy Spirit" (Rom. 15:13).

Faulty Belief: These emotions are so overwhelming I can't imagine ever getting over them.

Freedom Fact: God cares how I feel, and He has great compassion toward me. I can rest in knowing that He will carry my burdens.

Truth of Scripture: "Give all your worries and cares to God, for he cares about you" (1 Pet. 5:7, NLT). "Yet the Lord longs to be gracious to you; therefore, he will rise up to show you compassion. For the Lord is a God of justice" (Isa. 30:18). "For the Lord comforts his people and will have compassion on his afflicted ones" (Isa. 49:13).

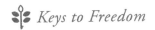 *Keys to Freedom*

Faulty Belief: People cannot be trusted, and I can expect to be betrayed.

Freedom Fact: God loves me, and I will trust Him no matter what. God will bring safe people into my life to love and encourage me in healthy ways.

Truth of Scripture: "Trust in the Lord with all your heart; do not depend on your own understanding" (Prov. 3:5, NLT). "To love him with all your heart, with all your understanding and with all your strength, and to love your neighbor as yourself is more important than all burnt offerings and sacrifices" (Mark 12:33). "If either of them falls down, one can help the other up. But pity anyone who falls and has no one to help them up" (Eccles. 4:10).

Faulty Belief: My coping methods are not that big of a deal and they don't really control me. Most people have little habits to help them get through the day anyway.

Freedom Fact: God has called me to a life of holiness that is no longer conformed to the patterns of the world and our culture. He has called me to focus my life and my mind on that which is good and pure.

Truth of Scripture: "'I have the right to do anything,' you say—but not everything is beneficial. 'I have the right to do anything'—but I will not be mastered by anything" (1 Cor. 6:12). "Do not conform to the pattern of this world, but be transformed by the renewing of your mind. Then, you will be able to test and approve what God's will is—his good, pleasing and perfect will" (Rom. 12:2). "Finally, brothers and sisters, whatever is true, whatever is noble, whatever is right, whatever is pure, whatever is lovely, whatever is admirable—if anything is excellent or praiseworthy—think about such things" (Phil. 4:8).

Faulty Belief: No one will ever want me. I am damaged goods.

Freedom Fact: God has taken my shame and restored me to wholeness. I have confessed my sin to Him, and He has forgiven me and cleansed me. I am a virgin in God's eyes. I have been set free to enjoy my future!

Truth of Scripture: "He has sent me to bind up the brokenhearted, to proclaim freedom for the captives and release from darkness for the prisoners, to proclaim the year of the Lord's favor and the day of vengeance of our God, to comfort all who mourn, and provide for those who grieve in Zion—to bestow on them a crown of beauty instead of ashes, the oil of joy instead of mourning, and a garment of praise instead of a spirit of despair. They will be called oaks of righteousness, a planting of the Lord for the display of his splendor" (Isa. -61:1–3). "I have loved you with an everlasting love; I have drawn you with unfailing kindness. I will build you up again, and you, Virgin Israel, will be rebuilt. Again you will take up your timbrels and go out to dance with the joyful" (Jer. 31:3–4). "Arise, my darling, my beautiful one, come with me. See! The winter is past; the rains are over and gone" (Song of Sol. 2:10–11).

Faulty Belief: No one—not even God—could ever love me after what I have been through.

Freedom Fact: God loves me unconditionally, and nothing can separate me from His unfailing love.

Truth of Scripture: "I have loved you with an everlasting love; I have drawn you with unfailing kindness" (Jer. 31:3). "For I am convinced that neither death nor life, neither angels nor demons, neither the present nor the future, nor any powers, neither height nor depth, nor anything else in all creation, will be able to separate us from the love of God that is in Christ Jesus our Lord" (Rom. 8:38–39). "Israel, put your hope in the Lord, for with the Lord is unfailing love and with him is full redemption" (Ps. 130:7).

Faulty Belief: I must hold myself together and not share how I feel.

Freedom Fact: God wants me to be real about how I feel, so He can provide comfort and healing. It is when I am healed and whole that I can comfort others who have been through the same things I have.

Truth of Scripture: "Blessed are those who mourn, for they will be comforted" (Matt. 5:4). "Praise be to the God and Father of our Lord Jesus Christ, the Father of compassion and the God of all comfort, who comforts us in all our troubles, so that we can comfort those in any trouble with the comfort we ourselves receive from God" (2 Cor. 1:3–4).

Faulty Belief: Since I was hurt by someone who was supposed to take care of me, no authority can be trusted.

Freedom Fact: I will choose to obey those in authority over me because I know God places people in authority for my protection and not to hurt or control me. I trust that God will protect me as I submit with a willing heart, and I know that those who misuse their authority will answer to Him.

Truth of Scripture: "Let everyone be subject to the governing authorities, for there is no authority except that which God has established. The authorities that exist have been established by God" (Rom. 13:1). "Whatever you do, work at it with all your heart, as working for the Lord, not for human masters, since you know that you will receive an inheritance from the Lord as a reward. It is the Lord Christ you are serving. Anyone who does wrong will be repaid for their wrongs, and there is no favoritism" (Col. 3:23–25). "Obey your earthly masters with respect and fear, and with sincerity of heart, just as you would obey Christ. Obey them not only to win their favor when their eye is on you, but as slaves of Christ, doing the will of God from your heart" (Eph. 6:5–6).

Faulty Belief: Sex is perverted and should never be enjoyed.

Freedom Fact: Sex was God's idea. God created a man and a woman to enjoy sex within the boundaries of marriage. It is a beautiful expression of love that I will one-day experience with my husband/wife.

Truth of Scripture: "So God created mankind in his own image, in the image of God he created them; male and female he created them. God blessed them and said to them, 'Be fruitful and increase in number; fill the earth and subdue it'" (Gen. 1:27–28). The entire book of the Song of Solomon is a great example of God celebrating appropriate sexuality.

Keys to Freedom

Faulty Belief: If I act like nothing ever happened, the memories and emotions will eventually go away.

Freedom Fact: I will speak out what is right, and I know God will be my refuge. I receive healing, so that I no longer live in fear but can experience true peace.

Truth of Scripture: "I will heal my people and will let them enjoy abundant peace and security" (Jer. 33:6). "Have nothing to do with the fruitless deeds of darkness, but rather expose them" (Eph. 5:11). "My inmost being will rejoice when your lips speak what is right" (Prov. 23:16). "The one whose walk is blameless is kept safe, but the one whose ways are perverse will fall into the pit" (Prov. 28:18).

Faulty Belief: I will get hurt and rejected if I open myself up. No one would really want to be my friend if they knew the real me.

Freedom Fact: With God's help, I can learn to be myself and trust Him to bring people into my life who will appreciate me and respect me for who I am. My worth is in who God says I am.

Truth of Scripture: "What's the price of two or three pet canaries? Some loose change, right? But, God never overlooks a single one. He pays even greater attention to you, down to the last detail—even numbering the hairs on your head! So, don't be intimidated by all this bully talk. You're worth more than a million canaries" (Luke 12:6–7, The Message). "God rescued us from dead-end alleys and dark dungeons. He's set us up in the kingdom of the Son he loves so much, the Son who got us out of the pit we were in, got rid of the sins we were doomed to keep repeating" (Col. 1:13–14, The Message).

Faulty Belief: If I am not perfect or "the best," I have failed.

Freedom Fact: I am fully loved, completely accepted, and totally pleasing to God. Regardless of how much I do or fail to do, I will remain fully loved, completely accepted, and totally pleasing to God. I choose to surrender to Him, trusting my faith in Him and His ability to sustain me. I will seek to be a God-pleaser, not a people-pleaser.

Truth of Scripture: "For I can do everything through Christ, who gives me strength" (Phil. 4:13, NLT). "Seek the Kingdom of God above all else, and live righteously, and he will give you everything you need" (Matt. 6:33, NLT).

Faulty Belief: My life has always been full of turmoil. Some of my best years have already been wasted.

Freedom Fact: God will restore all the time I have wasted or lost by my choices or the choices of others. God gives me peace.

Truth of Scripture: "I will restore to you the years that the swarming locust has eaten, the crawling locust, the consuming locust, and the chewing locust" (Joel 2:25, NKJV). "Peace I leave with you, My peace I give to you; not as the world gives do I give to you. Let not your heart be troubled, neither let it be afraid" (John 14:27, NKJV).

Appendix C
Daily Declarations

- I am a new creation in Christ Jesus. Old things have passed away and all things are new (2 Corinthians 5:17).
- I thank You that He who knew no sin became sin for me that I might be made the righteousness of God in Jesus Christ (2 Corinthians 5:21).
- God has not given me a spirit of fear, but of power, love, and a sound mind (2 Timothy 1:7).
- Lord, I choose to dedicate my body to You as a living sacrifice, and I will not conform to this world but will be transformed continually by the renewing of my mind (Romans 12:1-2).
- Lord, I have hidden Your Word in my heart that I might not sin against You (Psalm 119:11).
- The Lord has given me power and authority to tread on serpents and scorpions, and over all the power of the enemy, and nothing will hurt me (Luke 10:19).
- I am an overcomer, and I overcome by the blood of the Lamb and the word of my testimony (Revelation 12:1).
- Lord, I thank You that I am quick to hear (a ready listener); I am slow to speak, and I am slow to take offense and get angry (James 1:19).
- God is my refuge and my strength, a very present help in the time of trouble (Psalm 46:1).
- Because Jesus was tempted just like me, but never sinned, I will come boldly before His throne of grace to receive mercy and find help in my time of need (Hebrews 4:15-16).
- Lord I thank You that when I confess my sins, You are faithful and just to forgive me of my sins and to cleanse me from all unrighteousness (1 John 1:9).
- Because I choose to submit myself to God, I resist the devil and he flees from me (James 4:7).
- I am of God and have overcome Satan, for greater is He who is in me than he that is in the world (1 John 4:4).
- I will keep my way pure by conforming my life to the Word of God (Psalm 119:9).
- I will come to Jesus when I labor and am heavy laden, and He will give me rest. I will take His yoke upon me and learn from Him, for He is gentle and lowly in heart, and I will find rest for my soul. For His yoke is easy and His burden is light (Matt. 11:28-30).
- For God did not send His Son into the world to condemn the world, but that the world through Him might be saved (God's Word tells me that I am not condemned!) (John 3:17).
- I rejoice at Your Word as one who finds great treasure (Psalm 119:162).
- I will consider myself dead to sin and alive unto God (Romans 6:11).

- I will guard my mouth and my tongue so that I can keep my soul from trouble (Proverbs 21:23).
- For You, Lord, are good and ready to forgive, and abundant in mercy to all those who call upon You (So I will call upon You!)(Psalm 86:5).
- Be my strong refuge, to which I may resort continually; You have given the commandment to save me, for You are my rock and my fortress (Psalm 71:3).
- I will learn to do good, seek justice, rebuke the oppressor, defend the fatherless, and plead for the widow (Isaiah 1:17).
- Lord, You are my God. I will exalt You, I will praise Your name, for You have done wonderful things (Isaiah 25:1)!
- His grace is sufficient for me, for His strength is made perfect in my weakness. When I am weak, I will allow His strength and power to work in me (2 Corinthians 12:9).
- I will honor the Lord with my possessions, and with the first fruits of all my increase (Proverbs 3:9).
- I will dwell in the secret place of the Most High, I will abide under the shadow of the Almighty, and I will say of the Lord, "He is my refuge and my fortress; my God, in Him I will trust" (Psalm 91:1-2).
- As I live in God, love is being perfected in me, so that I may not be afraid in the day of judgment; because as He is, so am I in this world (1 John 4:17).
- There is no fear in love; but perfect love casts out all fear and torment. Because I have been perfected in love, I will not fear (1 John 4:18)!
- I will seek the Lord and His strength; I will seek His face forevermore (Psalm 105:4)!
- I will praise You, O Lord, with my whole heart; I will tell of all Your wonderful works (Psalm 9:1).
- I will be glad and rejoice in You; I will sing praise to Your name, O Most High (Psalm 9:2).
- The Lord is my rock and my fortress and my deliverer; my God, my strength in whom I will trust; my shield and the rock of my salvation, my stronghold (Psalm 18:2).
- I will bless the Lord at all times; His praise shall continually be in my mouth (Psalm 34:1).
- I will praise You, for I am fearfully and wonderfully made; marvelous are Your works, and that my soul knows very well (Psalm 139:14).
- I will delight myself in Your statutes; I will not forget Your word (Psalm 119:16).
- I will lie down in peace, and sleep; for You alone, O Lord, make me dwell in safety (Psalm 4:8).